Reading Prospect

Hideki Matsuo
Alexander A. Bodnar
Jay C. Stocker
Tsumoru Fujimoto

SANSHUSHA

音声ダウンロード＆ストリーミングサービス（無料）のご案内

https://www.sanshusha.co.jp/text/onsei/isbn/9784384335293/

本書の音声データは、上記アドレスよりダウンロードおよびストリーミング再生ができます。ぜひご利用ください。

はしがき

本書は、リーディング活動を支援し推進することを意図して編集された英文読解用のテキストで、2022年に刊行された*Reading Insight*などの続編となっています。トピックの点では、科学・技術系の問題に焦点を当てたものが多いものの、言語や建築、認知科学などのトピックも取り入れ、人文科学の分野に興味がある人にもできるだけ身近に感じてもらえるような題材で全体を構成しています。

語数は、どのユニットも400語から500語ぐらいまでと短めな英文で構成されていて、学習者ができるだけスムーズに取り組めるように、Unitの英文の量が少なめなものから多めなものになるように、また、内容が少し難しいと思われるUnitは後ろの方に配置しています。

各ユニットの英文に続くExercisesの A は、本文に出てきたkey wordsを確認するための語彙の問題と、本文の内容が理解できているかどうか、重要だと考えられている文の意味がとれているかどうか確認するための内容把握の問題です。 B には、TOEICに出てくるような英問英答の設問形式を使用しています。 C は、本文の内容を確認するためのTrue or Falseの問題です。 D は、英文に出てきた語句の使い方を確認するための問題で、 E は、英文に出てきた文法事項や構文を確認するための並べ替え問題です。 F には、本文の内容を確認するためにリスニングの問題を入れています。このように、総合的に英文読解力が養成できるようにExerciseの形式にバラエティを持たせています。また、問題の後に、コラムもつけ、英文中の事例の解説を行っています。

本書を通して、英文の内容を単に読み取ることだけではなく、英文の背景にあるものから学ぶ姿勢や、諸問題の持つさまざまな側面を考察する姿勢を涵養してもらいたいと考えています。*Reading Prospect*という本書の題名には、将来の展望を見据えてほしいという願いも込めています。本書が、そのような一助となれば幸いです。

2024年2月

松尾 秀樹 / Alexander A. Bodnar / Jay C. Stocker / 藤本 温

参考辞書一覧

Cambridge Advanced Learner's Dictionary (2008)
Cambridge Learner's Dictionary (2004)
Collins COBUILD Advanced Learner's English Dictionary (2006)
Longman Active Study Dictionary (2004)
Longman Dictionary of Contemporary English (2009)
Merriam-Webster's Advanced Learner's English Dictionary (2008)
Oxford Advanced Learner's Dictionary 10th edition (2020)
Oxford Learner's Dictionary of Academic English (2014)
Oxford Practical English Dictionary (2004)
カレッジライトハウス英和辞典、研究社 (1995)
英辞郎(第11版)、アルク (2020)

Contents

Unit 1 **Getting to the Roots of Meaning** 6
epidemic, pandemic, endemic の語源をたどる

Unit 2 **Cool Ideas...** 10
「熱さまシート」の開発経緯

Unit 3 **Happy Anniversary Snoopy: 50+ years of NASA and Peanuts Collaboration** 14
NASA とスヌーピーとのつながり

Unit 4 **Sweat the Details** 18
指紋認識精度を高める

Unit 5 **The Legacy of the *Rikejo*** 22
「リケジョ」の先駆者たち

Unit 6 **Rubik's Cube** 26
ルービックキューブの歴史について

Unit 7 **From Field to Fabulous: The Evolution of Kanazawa Station** 30
世界で最も美しい駅の1つとされている金沢駅について

Unit 8 **Zoom Fatigue** 34
オンラインコミュニケーションの弊害について

Unit 9 **Creating Sustainable Cities** 38
持続可能な都市づくりのために

Unit 10 **Kombu Will Save the World: Blue Carbon for a Healthier Planet** 42
ブルーカーボンとは？

Unit 11 **Is This Your Last Textbook?** 46
ChatGPT の教育に対する影響について

Unit 12 **Astro Boy and the DART Mission** 50
鉄腕アトムと NASA の DART ミッションについて

Unit 13 **Perceptions of Colors** 54
色の認識について

Unit 14 **Jumping to Conclusions** 58
結論に飛びつく私たちの認知の特性について

Unit 15 **Information Overload** 62
情報のオーバーロードへの対策

References 66

Unit 1

Getting to the Roots of Meaning

epidemic, pandemic, endemicの語源をたどる

新型コロナウィルスの世界的な流行とともに、pandemicという言葉は、すっかり聞きなれた言葉になりましたが、似たような言葉として、epidemicやendemicという言葉があります。この3つの言葉の語源をたどって共通点や違いを次の英文から読み取ってみましょう。

001

In recent years, we have had to deal with the coronavirus. The disease is bad enough, but navigating the terminology can also be confusing. Even native speakers of English sometimes need reminders. After all, the last pandemic was around a hundred years ago; and what exactly is a pandemic? Epidemic, pandemic, and endemic are all terms used to describe the spread of a disease, but they have different meanings based on their scale and location.

We can understand the differences more easily if we break the words down into different parts and find the origin behind their meaning. All three words contain the Greek root "dem," meaning "people." The prefixes "epi-," "pan-," and "en-" also have meanings.

Let's start with the word "epidemic." The prefix "epi-" means "among" or "on." An epidemic happens when a disease spreads quickly and affects many people in a certain area. It is usually caused by an infectious agent like a virus, bacteria, or parasite. The disease can spread easily when people are in close contact with each other. An example of an epidemic is a flu outbreak that may happen during the winter season.

"Pan-" in the word "pandemic" means "all." This appears in many words, such as "panorama." A panoramic photo is a 360 degree view showing everything in a scene. Similarly, a pandemic is a type of epidemic that affects people all over the world. It happens when a new virus or strain of a virus appears, and people do not have immunity to it. This means that the disease has spread all over the world. An example of a pandemic is COVID-19, which is still affecting people all over

terminology 術語、学術用語

reminder 思い出させる（呼び覚ます）ためのもの

infectious agent 感染症因子（病原体・病原菌）

parasite 寄生生物

outbreak 大流行

strain ここでは変異株のこと

the world. However, COVID-19 may have reached the endemic
30 stage.

The prefix "en" means "within" or "inside." It is also found in many words. For example, an email might have "enclosed" attachments such as pictures or documents. A more delicious example is almonds "enrobed" in chocolate. An
35 endemic disease is always present in a certain area or population. Most people who live in the area are used to the disease and have built up some immunity to it. Endemic diseases are caused by factors like the environment, genetics, or lifestyle. For example, malaria is endemic in Africa, while
40 dengue fever is endemic in Southeast Asia.

Hopefully, while reading the above explanation, you have not scratched your head too much and damaged your epidermis and endangered your health. In fact, maybe this is just the panacea for ensuring that you not only endure English in your
45 life but come to enjoy it more. (429 words)

enrobed 覆われた

genetics 遺伝的特徴
dengue fever デング熱

epidermis 表皮

panacea 万能薬、解決策

Exercises

A **設問に答えなさい。**

1. 次の語句の日本語の意味を答えなさい。

describe	contain	prefix	affect	immunity

2. Epidemic, pandemic, and endemic are all terms used to describe the spread of a disease, but they have different meanings based on their scale and location. (*l.* 5 ~ *l.* 8) を日本語に訳しなさい。

3. epidemic, pandemic, endemic について、1) それぞれの接頭辞の epi-, pan-, en- が持つ意味を答えなさい。また、2) それぞれどういう時に使われる用語であるか日本語で説明しなさい。さらに、3) それぞれの具体的な例を示しなさい。

1)

接頭語	epi-	pan-	en-
意味			

2)

epidemic	
pandemic	
endemic	

3)

epidemic	pandemic	endemic

B **本文の内容に合うように、質問の答えを選びなさい。**

1. What is a pandemic? (　　)

a) A disease that affects people all over the world.
b) A disease that is always present in a certain area or population.
c) A disease that spreads quickly and affects many people in a certain area.
d) A disease that spreads slowly and affects few people in a small area.

2. What is an epidemic? (　　)

a) A disease that is always present in a certain area or population.
b) A type of pandemic that affects people all over the world.
c) A disease that spreads quickly and affects many people in a certain area.
d) A disease caused by factors like the environment, genetics, or lifestyle.

C 本文の内容と一致しているものにはＴを、一致していないものにはＦを記入しなさい。

1. (　　) Epidemic, pandemic, and endemic all describe the spread of a disease.
2. (　　) An epidemic happens when a disease affects only a small area or population.
3. (　　) A pandemic is a type of epidemic that affects people all over the world.
4. (　　) Malaria is an example of a pandemic.
5. (　　) The prefix "pan-" means "all."
6. (　　) The prefix "epi-" means "within" or "inside."

D 次の各文の空欄に入る語句を右から選びなさい。

1. I like to stay in close (　　　　) with my parents.
2. They are preparing for an (　　　　) of the virus.
3. They have developed an (　　　　) to the virus.
4. Smoking increases the risk of heart (　　　　).
5. 'Multimedia' is the (　　　　) for any technique combing sounds and images.

term
contact
disease
immunity
outbreak

E 日本語に合うように与えられた語句を並べかえなさい。

They ____.

彼らはあなたが留守の時に電話をかけてきたかもしれない。

were / have / while / called / out / you / may

002–004

F 英文を聞いて、質問の答えをａ～ｃから選び記号で答えなさい。

1. What does the Greek root "dem" mean? (　　)
2. Which disease is endemic in Africa? (　　)
3. What does the prefix "en-" mean? (　　)

死者の埋葬

エンデミック、エピデミック、パンデミックのすべてに「デミック」という語が入っていますが、この「デム」はギリシア語の「デーモス」(民衆) に由来します。「デモクラシー (民主主義、民主制)」の場合も、もとのギリシア語「デモクラティアー」は「デーモス (民衆)」による国政の支配を意味します。現代イタリアの哲学者アガンベンは、この種の語源も意識して、COVID-19による感染拡大を政治的観点から考察して、死者を弔うことや移動の自由が感染拡大のリスクを回避するという名目で制限されたことを批判しました。葬式が行われないまま死者が葬られるということは、ソポクレスの悲劇『アンティゴネー』において、王クレオンがポリュネイケスの弔いを認めなかったこと、またそのときの妹アンティゴネーの胸中を想起させます。現代において、親しき人が葬儀や弔いなしに燃やされるという事態から、よく生きるという文化的・政治的な生と、生物学的な生存との分断をアガンベンは問うたわけです。

参考文献：ジョルジョ・アガンベン『私たちはどこにいるのか？―政治としてのエピデミック』高桑和巳訳、2021年、青土社

Cool Ideas...

額に貼る冷却シート「熱さまシート」が市販品として流通し始めたのは1994年のことですが、今や、年間約4億枚が売れている大ヒット商品となっているようです。「熱さまシート」の開発の経緯を次の英文から読み取ってみましょう。

005

Whenever there is a need, there is potential for a new product. One day, an employee at Kobayashi Pharmaceutical thought that there must be a better way to endure the heat produced by a fever. Often, feverish people will place a cool, wet towel on the forehead for relief. This can fall off easily, especially on children. After conducting a consumer survey, the company found there was a desire among consumers for a product that is ready to use quickly, does not slip off, and keeps cool for hours.

After two months of trial and error for the product, the eureka moment came when the leader of the project went to a tavern with a colleague. When reaching for a sashimi konnyaku, it landed on his hand. He thought to himself, "This is it!" The konnyaku was cool and pleasant to the touch. Inspired by that feeling, the researchers decided to develop a gel which could hold water and the technology to stick it to non-woven fabric.

Over 200 variations were made in the search for the perfect balance. Testing was done by researchers in a laboratory at 40 degrees Celsius with 75% humidity. They stuck the cooling pad on their foreheads for many hours every day to check how comfortable it was to use. One researcher even drank some alcohol to raise his body temperature.

When the product, Netsusama Sheet, was finally released in 1994, it was incredibly successful. Sales reached 5.5 million units, four times initial expectations. It was also a huge hit with Chinese tourists. In 2014, the Chinese media called it the "God medicine" and put it on its list of 12 medicines to buy

Kobayashi Pharmaceutical 小林製薬

eureka moment (研究などで)ピンときた瞬間

tavern 居酒屋

non-woven fabric 不織布

God medicine 日本に行ったら買わなければならない12の医薬品が「神薬」と呼ばれている。

when visiting Japan. Kobayashi Pharmaceutical followed up on this success by building a factory in China to supply the market there. Unexpectedly, the product also sold well in Japan in the summer. Many people were using it to keep cool on sweltering hot days. Today, the company sells about 400 million units a year in 20 countries.

sweltering
うだるように暑い

The president, Akihiro Kobayashi, says that innovation is the key to the continued success of his company. All employees are encouraged to submit ideas for new products. He says the company would not survive just by relying on its long-selling products. Those products rely on the domestic market which is shrinking due to the declining population of Japan. In 2022, about 40,000 product proposals were generated by employees.

Akihiro Kobayashi
小林章浩・小林製薬代表取締役社長

One of the company's new products is an ear warming plug which is designed to help people sleep. Time will tell how successful this product will be, but by the time you read this story, don't be surprised if you see another cool product on the market.

(449 words)

ear warming plug
小林製薬の商品名は「ナイトミン耳ほぐタイム」
睡眠を助けるように設計された耳を温める耳栓。

写真提供：小林製薬株式会社

Exercises

A 設問に答えなさい。

1. 次の語句の日本語の意味を答えなさい。

potential	endure	forehead	humidity	expectation

2. 「熱さまシート」のアイディアはどこでどういう時に生まれましたか。日本語で説明しなさい。

3. Inspired by that feeling, the researchers decided to develop a gel which could hold water and the technology to stick it to non-woven fabric. (*l.* 15 ~ *l.*17) を日本語に訳しなさい。

4. 小林製薬の社長が社員に言っていることはどういうことで、また、社員はどういうことを求められていますか。日本語で説明しなさい。

B 本文の内容に合うように、質問の答えを選びなさい。

1. What inspired the idea to use a gel in the Netsusama Sheet cooling pad? (　　)

a) A consumer survey　　b) A cool wet towel
c) A sashimi konnyaku　　d) A colleague's suggestion

2. How did the researchers test the comfort of the Netsusama Sheet product? (　　)

a) By sticking the cooling pad on their foreheads for many hours every day.
b) By using a survey among consumers.
c) By giving it to Chinese tourists.
d) By drinking some alcohol to raise body temperature.

C 本文の内容と一致しているものにはＴを、一致していないものにはＦを記入しなさい。

1. (　　) The company found that consumers were not interested in a product that relieves fevers.

2. (　　) The initial sales of Netsusama Sheet exceeded expectations.

3. (　　) The Netsusama Sheet was a hit with Chinese tourists in 2014.
4. (　　) Kobayashi Pharmaceutical built a factory in China to supply the Chinese market.
5. (　　) The president of Kobayashi Pharmaceutical believes that innovation is key to the company's continued success.
6. (　　) The ear warming plug is one of the company's best-selling products.

D 次の各文の空欄に入る語を右から選びなさい。

1. She (　　　　　) her report to the committee.
2. She (　　　　　) for the salt and pepper.
3. We (　　　　　) an opinion survey on the issue.
4. I (　　　　　) heavily upon your advice.
5. The book describes the hardships (　　　　　) by these immigrants.

reached
relied
submitted
endured
conducted

E 日本語に合うように与えられた語句を並べかえなさい。文頭に来るべき語も小文字になっています。

__________________________________, I __________________________________.

晴れた天気に触発されて、森を探索することにした。

explore / decided to / inspired / the woods / the sunny weather / by

006–008

F 英文を聞いて、質問の答えを a～c から選び記号で答えなさい。

1. How many variations of the Netsusama Sheet were made before its release? (　　)
2. How were the variations of the Netsusama Sheet tested? (　　)
3. What are all employees at Kobayashi Pharmaceutical encouraged to do? (　　)

Cool Ideas とは？

cool ideas という本ユニットのタイトルはどういう意味でしょうか。熱さまシートがテーマなので、おでこを「冷やす」とか「冷たい」という意味での cool ということはまずあるでしょう。本文の最後の方にある、cool product は、「なかなかしゃれた製品」という意味の cool で、この場合は「いけてる」というニュアンスでしょう。cool idea という言葉自体には「名案」という意味もあり、これは good idea と同義で、熱さまシートは名案だったというニュアンスもあるのかもしれません。日本語ではそれぞれ「冷たい」「なかなかしゃれた」「よい」と、あるいは「涼しい」「冷淡な」と訳し分けますが、英語では cool の一言で済むわけです。cool product を「冷たい製品」と訳してしまうと意味不明ですが、みなさんは、それがなぜ変なのかを英語を母語とするひとに説明できるでしょうか。言語は文化と密接に関わることを考えさせられます（参照 Unit 13）。

Unit 3 Happy Anniversary Snoopy: 50+ years of NASA and Peanuts Collaboration

NASAとスヌーピーとのつながり

2022年11月に行われたNASAの無人飛行の調査ミッション「アルテミス計画」に人気キャラクターのスヌーピーが乗り込みました。実は、NASAとスヌーピーとは、深いつながりがあるようです。次の英文からその関係を読み取ってみましょう。

009

The lovable comic character Snoopy has brought joy to millions of people for decades. Snoopy has also been a part of the enthusiasm surrounding NASA's human spaceflight missions for more than 50 years, encouraging future generations to have 5 great dreams. Charles M. Schultz and his beloved character Snoopy started their relationship with NASA in 1968 when Snoopy became the personal safety mascot for NASA astronauts. This partnership with the Peanuts character Snoopy continues to this day under the Artemis missions with new 10 educational initiatives.

Most recently, in November 2022, Snoopy served as Artemis I's zero gravity indicator. A zero gravity indicator is used onboard a spacecraft in order to provide a visual way of instantly knowing when the spaceship has entered the 15 weightlessness of microgravity; when Snoopy starts floating in the air, the spacecraft has reached zero gravity.

In the 1960s, during the era of the Apollo missions, Schulz drew comic strips titled "Snoopy on the Moon" to help create excitement for the space program. In May 1969, NASA 20 launched the Apollo 10 mission two months prior to the Apollo 11 mission, which made the first moon landing in July. The purpose of the Apollo 10 mission was to find a good landing spot for the Apollo 11 mission. The Apollo 10 lunar module skimmed 50,000 feet above the moon's surface. This action of 25 snooping around the moon's surface gave the crew the idea of nicknaming the lunar module "Snoopy." In addition, the command module was named "Charlie Brown," after Snoopy's loyal owner. Even the communication caps worn by the Apollo

Charles M. Schulz (1922-2000)
チャールズ·M·シュルツ(『ピーナッツ』の作者として知られているアメリカの漫画家)

the Artemis mission
アルテミス計画(ミッション)

zero gravity indicator
無重力インジケーター

microgravity
(宇宙船の中などの)微小重力(状態)

the lunar module
月着陸船

skim
〜の近くをかすめて飛ぶ

snoop around 〜
〜を(犬のように)探し回る

the command module
司令船

communication cap
宇宙飛行士がヘルメットの下にかぶっているキャップ

astronauts were called "Snoopy caps" because of their
30 noticeable black and white appearance. Snoopy himself, made his first trip into space in 1990, when he was able to board the Columbia space shuttle for the STS-32 mission.

These days, NASA astronauts show their gratitude to employees for their contributions to mission success and human
35 flight safety by awarding them the Silver Snoopy Award. The award includes a silver pin featuring astronaut Snoopy, which has been flown in space. The Artemis I mission also carried a package of Silver Snoopy pins for future recognitions.

In 2019, NASA and Peanuts Worldwide celebrated the 50th
40 anniversary of the Apollo 10 mission with a mini-documentary and educational materials aimed at inspiring the next generation of explorers. Peanuts also collaborated with McDonald's for a "Discover Space with Snoopy" Happy Meal. In addition, Peanuts, with its partner firm Wildbrain, premiered the first
45 season of "Snoopy in Space" on Apple TV+. Today, the partnership continues with a new curriculum and videos to encourage kids to learn about gravity, teamwork, and space exploration. Just as Snoopy was there when the first big steps were taken on the moon, he'll also be there for the next big
50 steps to come. (450 words)

the STS-32 mission
NASA のスペースシャトル計画のミッション名。STS = space transportation system

the Silver Snoopy Award
シルバー・スヌーピー賞

©NASA/George Homich

Wildbrain
カナダの映像制作会社

premiere
〜を放映する、（映画などを）封切る

season
テレビ番組で使われる用語

Apple TV+
アップルのオリジナル作品を楽しめるストリーミングサービス

©NASA/Isaac Watson

©NASA/Kim Shiflett

©Heather R. Smith/NASA Educational Technology Services

Exercises

A **設問に答えなさい。**

1. 次の語句の日本語の意味を答えなさい。

onboard	weightlessness	lunar	recognition	collaborate with ～

2. A zero gravity indicator is used onboard a spacecraft in order to provide a visual way of instantly knowing when the spaceship has entered the weightlessness of microgravity; when Snoopy starts floating in the air, the spacecraft has reached zero gravity. (*l.* 12～*l.* 16) を日本語に訳しなさい。

3. アポロ10号のミッションの主な目的は何でしたか。また、何に対して「スヌーピー」という名前を付けたのですか。またそれはどうしてですか。本文に沿って日本語で具体的に説明しなさい。

4. NASA は Peanuts Worldwide と共同でどういうことを行いましたか。日本語で説明しなさい。

B **本文の内容に合うように、質問の答えを選びなさい。**

1. What was the purpose of the Apollo 10 mission? (　　)

a) To take first samples of the lunar soil.
b) To make the first moon landing.
c) To test the durability of the lunar module.
d) To find a good landing spot for the Apollo 11 mission.

2. What is the Silver Snoopy Award? (　　)

a) An award given to NASA employees for their contributions to mission success and human flight safety.
b) An award given to Peanuts Worldwide for their collaboration with NASA.
c) An award given to astronauts who have flown in space.
d) A pin worn by the Apollo astronauts called "Snoopy caps."

C **本文の内容と一致しているものには T を、一致していないものには F を記入しなさい。**

1. (　　) Snoopy has been a part of NASA's human spaceflight missions for more than 50 years.

2. (　　) The Apollo 11 mission was the first mission to land on the moon.
3. (　　) The purpose of the Apollo 10 mission was to find a good landing spot for the Apollo 11 mission.
4. (　　) The Apollo 10 lunar module skimmed the moon's surface from 50 feet.
5. (　　) The Silver Snoopy Award includes a gold pin featuring astronaut Snoopy, which has been flown in space.
6. (　　) Snoopy was used as Artemis I's zero gravity indicator.

D 次の各文の(　　)の中に入る語を右から選びなさい。

1. The Navy is to (　　　　　) a new warship today.
2. The helicopter had to (　　　　　) an emergency landing.
3. The sofa had to (　　　　　) as a bed.
4. I strongly (　　　　　) everyone to go and see this important film.
5. The training programs (　　　　　) to raise employees' awareness of human rights.

encourage
aim
serve
make
launch

E 日本語に合うように与えられた語句を並べかえなさい。文頭に来るべき語も小文字になっています。

____.

第一段階が終わったら、ステップ2に進んでよい。

step 2 / you / completed / can / the first stage / , / having / move on to

F 英文を聞いて、質問の答えをa～cから選び記号で答えなさい。

010
|
012

1. What was Snoopy's recent role in the Artemis I mission? (　　)
2. What nickname did the Apollo 10 mission crew give to the lunar module? (　　)
3. What is the purpose of the Silver Snoopy Award? (　　)

スヌーピーでSTEM教育

本文の最後で、スヌーピーと教育について述べられていますが、スヌーピーが登場する日本語版の無料オンライン教材があります(対象は4～13歳)。まずはこのサイトを探してみてください。そこでは、漫画『ピーナッツ』に登場するスヌーピーをはじめとするキャラクターたちのふるまいを通してSTEMなどを学ぶことができます。STEMとは、Science(科学)、Technology(技術)、Engineering(工学)、Mathematics(数学)の頭文字をとったもので、中等・高等教育機関においても「STEM教育」として推奨されています。本ユニットの内容も、これら4つすべてに関わることは容易に理解できるでしょう。近年では、この4つにA(Arts)を加えた「STEAM教育」も提唱されており、このAには、芸術をはじめ、文化、経済、政治、倫理などが含まれ、文理融合的な学びも重視されるようになっています。

Unit 4

Sweat the Details

指紋認識精度を高める

指紋認証はスマートフォンなどにも搭載され、個人認証のために利用されています。誤認や偽造などの懸念もあるため、さらに精度を高めることをめざして、指の汗孔に着目した技術が開発されています。次の英文を読み、その開発の内容を読み取ってみましょう。

013

Keys are a part of our daily lives. They lock doors in homes, cars, and other places. Throughout history, people have also used keys to lock money or secret information in special boxes or cabinets. Today, you only need to use your finger to swiftly make an electronic payment or access private information stored on your smartphone. It's so convenient; unlike a key, you can't misplace your finger. You may be recognized everywhere using your fingerprint. However, whether using modern or older technologies, lock security is not always perfect. Even without a key, traditional locks can be picked and unlocked.

Fingerprint scanning technology is certainly amazing. The sensor recognizes patterns such as swirls and endpoints of lines in fingerprints. Unfortunately, smartphones are limited by their small scanner size. For instance, room entrances use larger scanners. The probability of misreading a fingerprint is one in a million. The chance of error on smartphones which have smaller sensors is one in 50,000.

Furthermore, the current technology is vulnerable to forgery. Researchers at the University of Michigan found that it's possible to print an image of a fingerprint and use that printout to unlock a smartphone. In Germany, Jan Krissler, also known by his hacker name, Starbug, used high resolution photos to successfully recreate the German defense minister's fingerprint. In a public demonstration, he showed that he could unlock her smartphone.

A new technology developed by researchers led by Professor Taizo Umezaki at the University of Tokyo and DDS, a biometric

pick (鍵を) こじ開ける

swirl 渦状紋

endpoint 線の端点

forgery 偽造

Jan Krissler ヤン・クリスラー（ドイツのコンピューター科学者・ハッカー）

Starbug スターバグ

Umezaki Taizo (1959-) 梅崎太造（中部大学理工学部 AI ロボテックス学科教授・東京大学大学院情報学環特任教授 [2015-2020]）

biometric 生体認証の

technology company, has made smartphone fingerprint
30 verification more secure and reliable. This technology uses sweat pores. Just like fingerprints, sweat pores are unique for every person. The process measures the distance from the pores in relation to the position of the lines in a fingerprint.

In order to identify these pores, DDS developed a new
35 scanner which combines a thin glass plate which is 0.6mm thick with an image sensor and light-emitting diode. This results in a resolution of 3,000 pixels per inch, a huge improvement over 500 ppi on existing scanners. At the moment, the new scanners are too expensive to compete with lower resolution scanners
40 which cost between 100 and 1,000 yen (93 cents to $9.30) each. With mass production, DDS expects the price to come down. The company plans to use this technology in the future for various other uses, including car and house locks.

In the movie *Catch Me If You Can*, Leonardo DiCaprio
45 plays the role of the elusive fraudster, Frank Abagnale, who cleverly finds ways to bypass security features. As long as there are locks to open and money to protect, there will likely be people like Abagnale using creative methods dishonestly. Looking forward, however, we can expect new devices which
50 are more secure and one step ahead of unscrupulous people.

(465 words)

sweat pore
汗孔（指の汗の出る穴）

light-emitting diode
発光ダイオード（LED）

ppi = pixels per inch
1インチ当たりの画素数を表す単位

Catch Me If You Can
スティーヴン・スピルバーグ監督の2002年映画。Frank Abagnaleの実話に基づいて作られている。

elusive
なかなか捕まらない

fraudster
詐欺師

Frank Abagnale
(1948-)
フランク・アバグネイル

bypass
～をすり抜ける

unscrupulous
不謹慎な

Exercises

A 設問に答えなさい。

1. 次の語句の日本語の意味を答えなさい。

misplace	vulnerable	secure	reliable	identify

2. ミシガン大学の研究者は、どういうことを見つけ出しましたか。日本語で説明しなさい。

3. the process (*l.32*) について、新しい技術では、何を測定して処理をするのですか。日本語で説明しなさい。

4. In order to identify these pores, DDS developed a new scanner which combines a thin glass plate which is 0.6mm thick with an image sensor and light-emitting diode. (*l.34 l.36*) を日本語に訳しなさい。

B 本文の内容に合うように、質問の答えを選びなさい。

1. How does smartphone fingerprint scanning technology currently work? (　　　)

a) A sensor recognizes patterns such as swirls, lines, and endpoints in a fingerprint.
b) A sensor forges patterns from a fingerprint.
c) A sensor makes 50,000 images from a fingerprint.
d) The software sends an image to a DDS database.

2. How can a hacker unlock another person's smartphone? (　　　)

a) By printing a copy of the owner's fingerprint.
b) By using a key to find the passcode.
c) By shaking hands with the owner of the smartphone.
d) By making a sensor from the owner's fingerprint.

C 本文の内容と一致しているものにはＴを、一致していないものにはＦを記入しなさい。

1. (　　) Traditional locks can be opened without the original key.

2. (　　) The chance of a smartphone making an error in correctly identifying a fingerprint is one in a million.

3. (　　) It's possible to unlock current smartphones by using a printed image of a fingerprint.

4. (　　) The new smartphone fingerprint scanning technology uses sweat pores to identify the user.
5. (　　) DDS created a new scanner with a resolution of 500 pixels per inch.
6. (　　) The price for the new DDS scanner is between 100 and 1,000 yen.

D 各文の空欄に入る語を右から選びなさい。

1. (　　　　) most systems, this one is very easy to install.
2. You can play football (　　　　) you do your homework first.
3. She can't eat dairy products (　　　　) milk and cheese.
4. Salaries are low (　　　　) the cost of living.
5. Eight people, (　　　　) two children, were injured in the explosion.

in relation to
including
unlike
as long as
such as

E 日本語に合うように与えられた語句を並べかえなさい。

It ____.

現金で払おうが小切手で払おうが関係ない。

pay / whether / by cash or check / matter / you / doesn't

F 英文を聞いて、質問の答えをa～cから選び記号で答えなさい。

014–016

1. What is the probability of a smartphone making a mistake in identifying a fingerprint correctly? (　　)
2. How many pixels per inch does the new DDS scanner measure? (　　)
3. What does the new fingerprint scanner recognize? (　　)

さまざまな認証方法

本人確認や認証のための初歩的な方法として、鍵やパスワード、印鑑や運転免許証、健康保険証、住民票などがあります。今日では新たな認証方法がいろいろと考案されて実際に使用されています。少し古い話ですが、2001年からアメリカでテレビ放映されたスパイアクションドラマ『エイリアス』では、顔認証や指紋認証のほかに、入り口で機器に息を吹きかける方法━生体認証━や、目の瞳孔をスキャンする方法━虹彩認証━がすでに登場していました。鍵は紛失や偽造の恐れがありますし、パスワードは忘却したり盗まれることもあり得ます。指紋や息や虹彩は本人から切り離せないもので、紛失や忘却はないことから安全性や信頼性は高いように思います。そうしたメリットがある反面、デメリットはないのでしょうか。たとえば、エラーの可能性や、開発や導入のコストはどうなのでしょうか。新たな認証方法それぞれのメリットとデメリットについてみなさんで考えてみてください。

Unit 5

The Legacy of the *Rikejo*

「リケジョ」の先駆者たち

理工系に進む女子学生の比率はいまだ低いと言われています。次の英文は、戦中・戦後、東京工業大学で学んだ２人の女性の話についてです。女性が学んだり働いたりする上での当時の社会環境の一端を英文から読み取ってみましょう。

017

Obtaining a university degree may not seem like a major obstacle for many women nowadays, but that was not the case until the latter half of the 20th century. In fact, it was almost unthinkable at the beginning of the 1900s. Throughout subsequent years, women have had to work very hard to prove that they are just as capable as men in the world of academics. This is especially true for the study of the "hard" sciences, which is an area still dominated by men. We will take a look at some of the pioneering "*Rikejo*" (women in science) in Japan.

So who were these pioneers, and what motivated them to pursue a higher education in the sciences against difficulties almost impossible to overcome? One of these women was Sada Orihara, the first female student to enter and graduate from Tokyo Institute of Technology. She obtained a scholarship to study in the Department of Dye Chemistry in 1931. Among about 150 students who entered Tokyo Tech that year, she was the only female student.

After graduating, she resumed teaching at Tokyo Women's Higher Normal School. Orihara married Kiyoshi Takiura, one of her classmates at Tokyo Tech, in 1939, and gave birth to a son. If you think taking care of a family and working full-time is difficult today, just imagine how difficult it was for her in wartime Japan. Her husband was transferred to the Kansai region in 1943 when her son was just a toddler. Orihara remained in Tokyo and had to bring her son to work every day, as there were no childcare facilities in those days. Her son would play under her desk while she lectured.

Another pioneering college woman, Michiko Togo, entered

the "hard" sciences
ここでは工学も含めた自然科学の分野のことを指している。

Rikejo
理工系の分野で活躍する女性の略称。

Sada Orihara
(1908-60) 折原さだ

the Department of Dye Chemistry
染料化学科

Tokyo Women's Higher Normal School
東京女子高等師範学校

Kiyoshi Takiura
(1911-94) 瀧浦潔

toddler
よちよち歩きの幼児

Michiko Togo
(1927-2018) 十合（とうごう）道子

Tokyo Tech in 1947. She came from two generations of
30 scientists. Her maternal grandfather, Kunihiko Iwadare, founded NEC Corporation, and her father graduated from Tokyo Tech. She desperately wanted to become an engineer in order to contribute to Japan's postwar recovery. Her determination helped her pass the difficult and competitive
35 entrance exam. However, she experienced culture shock after she started to attend classes on campus as the only female student. She experienced some embarrassment concerning the absence of a woman's bathroom, so she asked her academic supervisor to have a sign saying "women only" on one
40 bathroom door. After graduating, she continued her studies in the United States for two years. Upon returning to Japan, she married a pastor and supported him with his missionary activities.

The position of women in society has risen considerably
45 since the days of pioneers like Sada Orihara and Michiko Togo. Thanks to the resilience and hard work of these and many other *Rikejo*, more and more women are able to pursue careers in scientific fields today. It is important to remember their efforts and sacrifices. (467 words)

maternal
母方の
Kunihiko Iwadare
(1857-1941) 岩垂邦彦

pastor
牧師
missionary activities
布教活動

resilience
(困難・苦境から) 立ち直る力、
(それらを) 跳ね返す力

折原さださんと瀧浦潔さん

十合道子さん

写真提供：東京工業大学博物館

Exercises

A 設問に答えなさい。

1. 次の語句の日本語の意味を答えなさい。

pursue	embarrassment	resume	contribute	sacrifice (*n.*)

2. Obtaining a university degree may not seem like a major obstacle for many women nowadays, but that was not the case until the latter half of the 20th century. (*l.* 1 ~ *l.* 3)
を日本語に訳しなさい。

3. 折原さださんは、当時どういうところに苦労されたと述べてありますか。本文に沿って日本語で説明をしなさい。

4. 十合(とうごう)道子さんは、当時どういうところに苦労されたと述べてありますか。本文に沿って日本語で説明をしなさい。

B 本文の内容に合うように、次の質問の答えを選びなさい。

1. What was the example of culture shock mentioned in the article? (　　)

a) There were few good childcare facilities in those days.
b) There were about the same number of female students studying at the school as the male students.
c) There was no women's bathroom.
d) There weren't any women pursuing a higher education in science.

2. Why did Michiko Togo want to become an engineer? (　　)

a) Because she came from three generations of scientists.
b) Because she wanted to contribute to Japan's postwar recovery.
c) Because she got a scholarship to study engineering at Tokyo Tech.
d) Because she passed the difficult and competitive entrance exam.

C 本文の内容と一致しているものにはTを、一致していないものにはFを記入しなさい。

1. (　　) It was common for women to obtain a university degree in the early 1900s.
2. (　　) The study of the "hard" sciences is an area still dominated by men.
3. (　　) Sada Orihara was the first female student to study at Tokyo Tech.
4. (　　) It was easier for women to take care of a family and work full-time in wartime Japan than it is today.
5. (　　) Michiko Togo wasn't concerned about the absence of a women's bathroom at the school.
6. (　　) Michiko Togo's paternal grandfather founded NEC Corporation.

D 各文の空欄に入る語を右から選びなさい。

contribute
resume
help
transfer
pursue

1. Come and (　　　　) me lift this box.
2. She wishes to (　　　　) a medical career.
3. He did not (　　　　) to the project.
4. She hopes to (　　　　) work after the baby is born.
5. I'll be upstairs, so could you (　　　　) my phone calls up there, please?

E 日本語に合うように与えられた語句を並べかえなさい。

If ________________________________, we need more staff.

もしそれが事実なら、もっとスタッフが必要だ。

case / is / the / that

F 英文を聞いて、質問の答えをa～cから選び記号で答えなさい。

018–020

1. What did Sada Orihara obtain to study at Tokyo Tech? (　　)
2. What year did Michiko Togo enter Tokyo Tech? (　　)
3. According to the article, what is important to remember about the *Rikejo*? (　　)

「多様性」について考える

「リケジョ」の話は、女性の社会進出や男女共同参画としての意味もありますが、より広く言えば、「ダイバーシティ」(diversity)の議論に繋がります。ダイバーシティとは、性別のみならず、人種、宗教、障がい等による差別がないことであり、多様な生き方や考え方を社会が受け容れていくことです。「生物多様性」も、一言でいうと、多様な生物がいた方がよいということで、今日、多様性の重要性がしばしば説かれています。その反対はもちろん多様性を認めない一様な見方です。ナチスの時代には、優生学的思想に基づいて、障がい者の消滅を意図した断種法が施行されたことがありました。政治においても、実質的に一つの政党しか機能していない社会でみなさんは暮らしたいでしょうか。多様性を認めるべきであるという考え方について、また、その方が全体として社会はうまく機能するだろうという見方について、「リケジョ」の話を含めてみなさんで意見交換を行ってみてください。

Unit 6

Rubik's Cube

ルービックキューブの歴史について

ルービックキューブは、世界中の何百万人もの人々が楽しんでいると言われているおもちゃですが、誰によってどうやって作られたかはあまり知られていないようです。次の英文を読み、ルービックキューブの歴史を読み取ってみましょう。

021

It has been almost 50 years since the debut of the Rubik's Cube. Although it is a very popular toy that has been used by millions of people around the world, very few people are aware of its humble origins.

Ernő Rubik (1944-)
エルノー・ルービック

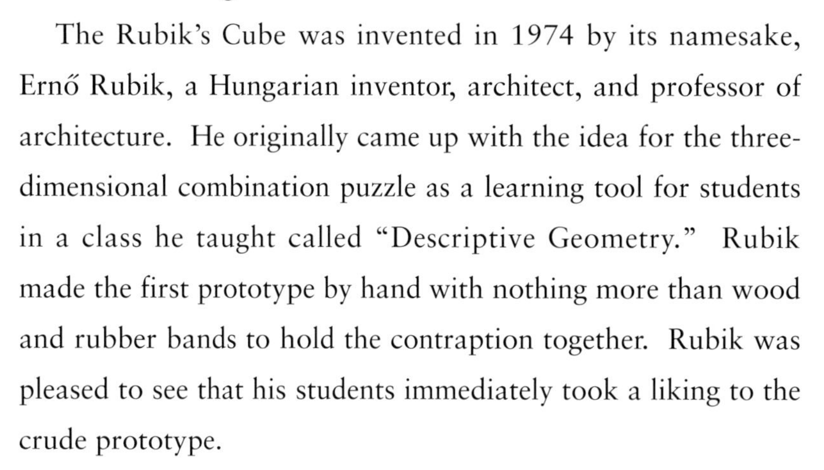

The Rubik's Cube was invented in 1974 by its namesake, Ernő Rubik, a Hungarian inventor, architect, and professor of architecture. He originally came up with the idea for the three-dimensional combination puzzle as a learning tool for students in a class he taught called "Descriptive Geometry." Rubik made the first prototype by hand with nothing more than wood and rubber bands to hold the contraption together. Rubik was pleased to see that his students immediately took a liking to the crude prototype.

descriptive geometry 記述幾何学

contraption からくり、発明品

take a liking to～ ～を好きになる

crude 大雑把な、未完成の

Rubik realized that because of the simple construction, it would be easy to manufacture. After obtaining a patent for the device, he set out to find a manufacturer in Hungary to mass-produce it. This proved to be difficult because of the inflexible planned economy of communist Hungary at that time. After an exhaustive search, he found a small manufacturing company in Hungary that made plastic chess pieces. They agreed to initially produce 5,000 of the devices made entirely of plastic.

communist 共産主義の

The cube was originally known as the Magic Cube, and it had limited distribution mainly in Hungary and then in the United Kingdom under contract to a company called Pentangle Puzzles. Hungary was behind the Iron Curtain at the time, and exports were strictly controlled. Unsatisfied with the slow pace of sales in limited markets, Rubik decided to attend international toy fairs on his own volition. One day at the

the Iron Curtain 鉄のカーテン（第二次世界大戦後の旧ソ連圏と西欧諸国との間の障壁）

volition 意志

Nuremberg Toy Fair in Germany, he met Tom Kremer, a
30 marketer for an American toy company. Kremer was so taken by the strange toy that he decided on the spot to bring it to America.

Ideal Toy Company was the name of the company that Kremer worked for. They rebranded the cube as the Rubik's
35 Cube, which is the name that has been used for it ever since. It became an instant hit after it was introduced internationally to the public in 1980. There have been over 450 million Rubik's Cubes sold worldwide since then.

So, how long does it take for you to solve the cube? Many
40 people give up in frustration after their first attempt to solve it. To date, the fastest person to ever solve the standard 3x3x3 Rubik's Cube is Max Park of the USA with a blistering speed of 3.13 seconds on June 11 2023.

Recently, researchers deciphered the standard 3x3x3 Rubik's
45 cube, calculating that the cube could be solved from any of the 43 quintillion possible orientations in 20 moves or less. Do you have what it takes to solve the puzzle in record time?

(463 words)

Nuremberg ニュルンベルク（ドイツの都市名）
Tom Kremer (1930-2017) トム・クレマー
blistering 非常に速い
decipher 読み解く
quintillion 10の18乗、100京
orientation 幾何学的配置
have what it takes to～ ～する素質がある、～する才能がある
in record time 記録的な速さで

Exercises

A **設問に答えなさい。**

1. 次の語句の日本語の意味を答えなさい。

patent (*n.*)	device	unsatisfied	worldwide	to date

2. エルノー・ルービック氏によって開発された最初のルービックキューブはどういうものでしたか。日本語で説明しなさい。

3. 最初あまり広まらなかったルービックキューブが世界的に広まるようになったきっかけはどういうことでしたか。日本語で説明しなさい。

4. There have been over 450 million Rubik's Cubes sold worldwide since then. (*l.37*〜*l.38*) を日本語に訳しなさい。

B **本文の内容に合うように、次の質問の答えを選びなさい。**

1. What did Rubik use to make his first prototype of the cube? (　　)

a) Plastic　b) Metal　c) Chess pieces　d) Wood and rubber bands

2. What is the name of the company that first distributed the Magic Cube in the United Kingdom? (　　)

a) Magic Cube Incorporated　b) Ideal Toy Company
c) Pentangle Puzzles　d) Rubik's Cube International Ltd.

C **本文の内容と一致しているものにはＴを、一致していないものにはＦを記入しなさい。**

1. (　　) The very first prototype of the cube was made by a small manufacturing company in Hungary.

2. (　　) Rubik thought the cube would be easy to manufacture because of its simple construction.

3. (　　) The cube was originally known as the Magic Cube.

4. (　　) Rubik met Tom Kremer at a toy fair in America.
5. (　　) It has been proven that the cube can be solved in 20 moves or less.
6. (　　) Rubik obtained a patent for the cube after he found a manufacturer for the device.

D 次の各文の空欄に入る語を右から選びなさい。語形は変化させる必要がある場合があります。

1. We've been asked to (　　　　　) some new ideas.
2. He (　　　　　) become a lawyer but ended up teaching history instead.
3. The new drug may (　　　　　) be effective.
4. Why don't you (　　　　　) smoking?
5. She (　　　　　) an engineering company.

prove to
work for
set out to
come up with
give up

E 日本語に合うように与えられた語句を並べかえなさい。

By ____.

私が帰ってくるまでには、食事が残っていなかった。

no food / left / , / I / there / the time / got back / was

F 英文を聞いて、質問の答えを a 〜 c から選び記号で答えなさい。

022
|
024

1. What is the current world record for solving the standard 3x3x3 Rubik's Cube?
(　　)
2. What year was the Rubik's Cube introduced to the public internationally?
(　　)
3. How many cubes were initially produced by the manufacturing company in Hungary?
(　　)

娯楽の役割

ルービックキューブのような何百万もの人々が楽しめるおもちゃは今後はあまり登場しないように思います。スマホや PC のゲームがなかった時代においては、ルービックキューブにトライする子供や大人は多かったでしょう。近年ではゲームの種類が豊富になり、次々と新たなゲームや遊具が開発されて消費され、消えていきます。映画や本にしても大量の作品が次々と制作されて、長く残る名作や名品が生まれにくくなっています。娯楽の役割のひとつには、同じ映画や本について友人たちと語り合うこと、つまりコミュニケーションということもあるはずですが、近年では個人の趣味が多様化しているため、自分と同じ映画や本やゲームに興味がある友人が周りにいないことも多いでしょう。コミュニケーションの重要性がしばしば指摘される一方、娯楽を通じてのコミュニケーションの機会は残念ながら減っており、娯楽のもつ意味や役割も変化してきているようです。

Unit 7

From Field to Fabulous: The Evolution of Kanazawa Station

世界で最も美しい駅の１つとされている金沢駅について

金沢駅は、建築の造形の美しさの代表とされていて、アメリカの旅行誌の「世界で最も美しい駅14選」に選ばれているそうです。金沢駅の建築物としてのコンセプトを次の英文から読み取ってみましょう。

025

From a bare, plain field to a modern urban beauty. Kanazawa Station is considered one of the most beautiful stations in the world according to various travel websites. Kanazawa Station had simple beginnings, but for more than a century, it grew and expanded while respecting tradition.

The station opened for the first time in 1898, when the Hokuriku Rail Line was extended from Fukui. At that time, the station was a simple one-story wooden building surrounded by fields. Instead of taxis, rickshaw runners picked up passengers arriving by train. By 1945, the station had become old and worn out with 28,300 passengers passing through daily, 14 times more volume compared to when it first opened. It was no longer suitable as a gateway to the growing city. Despite the dire need for an update, the national government prioritized rebuilding destroyed stations between Tokyo and Kobe after the end of the Second World War. With local community support, the second era of Kanazawa Station began with new construction in 1951 and was completed in 1953. It was a four-story structure made from concrete and reinforced steel. It was quite modern for the time and had 44 shops.

In order to accommodate the new bullet train route, it was necessary to upgrade the station once more in the late 1990s. A significant renovation started in 1998 and was finished in 2005. Modernizing historic buildings can sometimes disconnect them from their past. In contrast, architect Ryuzo Shirae's aesthetically pleasing design highlights Kanazawa's history and culture, making it unique among Japanese train stations.

Whereas in most stations you would see ordinary posts and

the Hokuriku Rail Line 北陸鉄道

rickshaw 人力車

dire 差し迫った

Ryuzo Shirae (1952-) 白江 龍三（日本の建築家）

beams, Kanazawa Station's central concourse has a series of
30 beams and pillars made of wood. These resemble torii gates
seen at shrines. There are 12 of these gates, each supported by
two pillars made of native cypress wood. If you look closely at
them, you will notice that each one contains a beautiful work
of art. These works of art showcase the lacquerware,
35 woodwork, and ceramic crafts of Kanazawa's past.

The most impressive part of the station is the massive
wooden torii gate at the entrance. At first glance, it looks like
two pillars made from a twisted arrangement of giant match
sticks. In fact, the pillars are shaped to resemble tsuzumi, a
40 type of drum used in Noh theater, which is why it's called
Tsuzumi-mon or Tsuzumi Gate. This natural and historic
element blends magnificently with the Omotenashi Dome made
of aluminum and glass. Not only is it aesthetically pleasing, it's
also practical. It offers protection from rain and snow, truly
45 hospitable as suggested by the name.

From simple origins, this modern station has put Kanazawa
on the world map with its postcard-worthy design. This
gateway to the past awaits you only 2.5 hours by rail from
Tokyo. (468 words)

cypress wood
ヒノキ材

showcase
～を目立つように見せている

lacquerware
漆細工

Exercises

A 設問に答えなさい。

1. 次の語句の日本語の意味を答えなさい。

disconnect	highlight (*v.*)	beam	pillar	blend (*v.*)

2. 金沢駅が1898年にオープンした時の駅舎はどんな感じでしたか。日本語で説明しなさい。

3. 現在の金沢駅の一番印象的な部分は、どこで、どんな風に見えると述べてありますか。日本語で説明しなさい。

4. Not only is it aesthetically pleasing, it's also practical. (*l.* 43 ~ *l.* 44) を日本語に訳しなさい。

B 本文の内容に合うように、質問の答えを選びなさい。

1. What was the priority of the national government in Japan after the end of the Second World War? (　　)

a) To modernize Kanazawa Station.
b) To rebuild stations between Tokyo and Kobe.
c) To preserve the history and culture of Kanazawa Station.
d) To construct a new four-story building with reinforced steel.

2. What is the design of Kanazawa Station's central concourse like? (　　)

a) It is made of ordinary posts and beams.
b) It is made of a series of beams and pillars resembling torii gates seen at shrines.
c) It is a modern design made of aluminum and glass.
d) It is a simple one-story wooden building.

C 本文の内容と一致しているものにはTを、一致していないものにはFを記入しなさい。

1. (　　) The station was first built as a four-story concrete structure.

2. (　　) The architect's design of the station highlights Kanazawa's history and culture.

3. (　　) The central concourse of Kanazawa Station has ordinary posts and beams made from imported maple wood.
4. (　　) The 12 torii gates in the central concourse contain beautiful works of art.
5. (　　) The pillars of the torii gate at the entrance are shaped to resemble a type of drum used in Noh theater.
6. (　　) The Omotenashi Dome is made of wood and glass.

D 次の各文の空欄に入る語句を右から選びなさい。文頭に来るべき語句も小文字になっています。

1. It's (　　　　　) a secret.
2. Today's quiz was easy (　　　　　) the last one.
3. (　　　　　) our objections, he insisted on driving.
4. (　　　　　) to last year's profits, the company is not doing very well.
5. The old system was fairly complicated, (　　　　　) the new system is really simple.

whereas
no longer
in contrast
despite
compared to

E 日本語に合うように与えられた語句を並べかえなさい。文頭に来るべき語も小文字になっています。

____.

こんな音が鳴り続けている状況では私は宿題をできない。
my homework / all this noise / I / with / can't / going on / do

F 英文を聞いて、質問の答えを a 〜 c から選び記号で答えなさい。

026–028

1. What was the original building of Kanazawa Station made of? (　　)
2. What material is used to make the Omotenashi Dome? (　　)
3. How long does it take to get to Kanazawa Station from Tokyo by train? (　　)

金沢駅の「鼓門」

金沢では伝統芸能である能楽が親しまれてきました。金沢駅の「鼓門(つづみもん)」は、能楽の鼓をイメージしていると言われています。能は神社の能舞台で行われましたので、鼓門には神聖な領域に足を踏み入れるときに通る鳥居のような意味づけがあるのでしょう。金沢は伝統的に仏教の盛んな地域でもあり、仏教関連では、戦国時代の1546年頃に建立された金沢御坊―尾山御坊(おやまごぼう)とも呼ばれます―は一向一揆の拠点で、現在は金沢城址公園となっています。金沢は加賀藩前田家14代が約300年間つづいた城下町であり、寺院の他にも、武家屋敷、商家、坂道と水路などの跡が残されています。鼓門の完成(2005年)の後、2015年に金沢―長野間で新幹線が開通したことから、「鼓門」は現在では、新幹線を利用した旅行者が上記の歴史や文化に触れる「門」の役割をも担っていることになるでしょう。

Unit 8

Zoom Fatigue

オンラインコミュニケーションの弊害について

コロナ禍によって、リモートワークやオンライン授業などは日常的なものになっていますが、とても便利な面がある一方で、弊害も出てきているようです。どういう弊害があるのか、またその原因は何なのか、英文から読み取ってみましょう。

029

Ever since the COVID-19 pandemic swept across the globe, millions of people have had to work from home using video conferencing tools. Although working remotely can be convenient and safe for many workers, there are several 5 drawbacks to extended use of applications like Zoom, Skype, Google Meet, or FaceTime. One major problem is the general feeling of exhaustion that many people experience after prolonged use of video conferencing tools. In fact, the problem has become so pervasive that it has taken on the new term, 10 "Zoom fatigue."

So, why do so many people become exhausted after protracted use of applications like Zoom? It appears to have a lot to do with our dependence on nonverbal communication and vocal cues. Albert Mehrabian, a renowned researcher of 15 body language, found that conveying emotions, such as anger or happiness, is 55% nonverbal, 38% vocal, and 7% words only. In face-to-face communication, perceiving these cues comes naturally to most people, taking little conscious effort to interpret correctly. However, video conferencing impairs these 20 ingrained abilities, requiring sustained and intense attention to the verbal message, which is very taxing on the brain. If the video or audio quality is poor, or if the person is not facing the camera directly, picking up facial expressions and voice intonation can be next to impossible.

25 Many researchers have begun to study the problem of Zoom fatigue. A group of researchers at Stanford University created a tool to measure it, which they named the Zoom Exhaustion & Fatigue Scale, or ZEF. One study gathered over 10,000

COVID-19
新型コロナウィルス感染症 (Corona Virus Infectious Disease, emerged in 2019 に由来している)

protracted
長引いた

Albert Mehrabian
(1939-) アルバート・メラビアン（アメリカの心理学者）

ingrained
染み付いた

taxing
ひどく負荷がかかる

responses on a survey that measured people's fatigue on the
30 ZEF scale. It also collected statistics about how long each
person spent on Zoom, along with demographic information.
The data collected clearly showed that spending more time on
video calls, with very little time between calls, caused more
Zoom fatigue. The data also identified four factors that
35 teleworkers have to cope with when using video conferencing.

First of all, the lack of nonverbal cues is stressful because
people cannot naturally convey or interpret gestures and body
language when just the shoulders and heads are visible.
Secondly, during video calls people report feeling trapped in one
40 spot so that they can stay within view of the webcam, increasing
stress levels. Thirdly, many video conferencing tools default to
showing users their own video windows. The researchers found
that this constant, real-time reflection can cause what's known
as mirror anxiety, which can lead to increased stress and
45 depression. Finally, many people mention an intense feeling
that the other people on the call are staring at them, as if they
are standing less than two feet away. This kind of physical
proximity is very uncomfortable for many people, which leads
to increased stress levels.

50 Although working remotely has many advantages, it is
important to be aware of the problems workers can face when
using online conferencing tools. Employers and their staff need
to work together to find solutions to these problems. (493 words)

demographic information 人口統計学的情報

default ～をデフォルトに（規定値に設定）する

mirror anxiety 鏡の不安

Exercises

A 設問に答えなさい。

1. 次の語句の日本語の意味を答えなさい。

fatigue	drawback	pervasive	convey	impair

2. One major problem is the general feeling of exhaustion that many people experience after prolonged use of video conferencing tools. (*l.* 6 ~ *l.* 8) を日本語に訳しなさい。

3. Albert Mehrabian 氏は、感情を相手に伝える時の要素としてもっとも割合の大きいものは何だと述べていますか。日本語で答えなさい。

4. Stanford 大学の ZEF の調査によってわかった Zoom fatigue を起こす4つの要因について、それぞれ日本語でまとめなさい。

・

・

・

・

B 本文の内容に合うように、質問の答えを選びなさい。

1. What is the term used to refer to the stress some people feel when looking at their own image in a video conference? (　　)

a) Mirror anxiety　　b) Zoom fatigue
c) Zoom Exhaustion　　d) Nonverbal cues

2. What is the best definition of "Zoom fatigue?" (　　)

a) The feeling of anxiety one gets from not being able to work at the office.
b) The general feeling of exhaustion after prolonged use of video conferencing tools.
c) The dependence on nonverbal communication and vocal cues.
d) The sustained and intense attention to the verbal message while video conferencing.

C 本文の内容と一致しているものには T を、一致していないものには F を記入しなさい。

1. (　　) Only people who use Zoom experience Zoom fatigue.

2. (　　) There are no advantages to working remotely.

3. (　　) Zoom fatigue seems to have a lot to do with our dependence on nonverbal communication and vocal cues.
4. (　　) One factor some teleworkers have to deal with is mirror anxiety.
5. (　　) Video conferencing requires sustained and intense attention to the verbal message.
6. (　　) Perceiving nonverbal communication and vocal cues is not difficult for most people to do when video conferencing.

D 各文の空欄に入る語を右から選びなさい。

1. A degree in English could (　　　　　) to a career in journalism.
2. He wasn't able to (　　　　　) with the stresses and strains of the job.
3. Smoking can (　　　　　) your health.
4. The chameleon can (　　　　　) on the colors of its background.
5. I didn't know whether to (　　　　　) her silence as acceptance or refusal.

impair
interpret
lead
cope
take

E 日本語に合うように与えられた語句を並べかえなさい。

She ____.

彼女はとても疲れていたので、まともに頭が働かなかった。

that / couldn't / was / think straight / she / tired / so

F 英文を聞いて、質問の答えを a ～ c から選び記号で答えなさい。

030–032

1. What was not mentioned as being a video conferencing tool people use? (　　)
2. Who created the Zoom Exhaustion and Fatigue Scale (ZEF)? (　　)
3. According to Albert Mehrabian, what percentage of communicating emotions is verbal? (　　)

オンライン会議の疲労解決法は？

COVID-19の流行以後、これほどオンライン会議が一般的になると、以前の対面会議に完全に戻ることは難しいはずです。オンライン会議でなぜ疲れるのか。本ユニットでは4つの要因が挙げられていますが、おそらく他にも原因があって、今後、研究が進んでいくことでしょう。原因を突き止めた後には、それらを解消・解決するための方策を考えなければなりません。画面上で多くの人々に見られている感覚が長時間続くことへのストレスに対しては、会議の合間に休憩時間を多く入れるとか、一定時間は画面非表示で会議を実施するという対策が考えられます。非言語的な合図の欠如、つまり、オンラインでは身振りを通して意思伝達が難しいという点については、何かよい方策はあるでしょうか。"Zoom fatigue"を軽減する方策をみなさんも考えてみてください。いずれオンライン会議疲労を軽減する画面の開発や疲労抑制グッズ、疲労回復グッズなども登場するかもしれませんね。

Unit 9 Creating Sustainable Cities

持続可能な都市づくりのために

持続可能な都市づくりのためには、処理費用にコストがかかる廃棄物を有効活用し、貴重な資源に変えることが求められています。次の英文を読み、いくつかの都市の取り組みについて読み取ってみましょう。

You may have heard of the 3Rs of sustainability: reduce, reuse and recycle. These are important steps to follow to minimize the impacts of pollution on our urban environments. But no matter how efficient our systems are, there will still be waste. In order to create a sustainable city, it is crucial to convert the remaining waste into usable resources. In this way, waste from one process becomes raw material for another, thereby creating a closed loop of sustainability.

Most cities are full of wasted resources; such as wasted energy, wasted carbon dioxide, wasted food, and wasted water. Reducing each waste stream and managing it as a resource — rather than a cost — can solve multiple problems at once, thereby creating a more sustainable future for the billions of people that live in these urban areas around the world.

How can we close these loops and use our wasted resources in beneficial ways? Our solutions are only limited by our ability to use our imaginations. Vancouver is one city that has taken concrete steps to implement innovative solutions to sustainability issues. The city has pledged to become the greenest city on earth. They gave every resident separate bins for trash and organic matter. The city produces methane from the organic waste and burns it to heat nearby greenhouses that grow tomatoes. They produce solids (known as amendments) from the remaining waste that is added to the soil to improve the tomatoes.

Austin, Texas, is another city that does something similar with its wastewater sludge. They pass it through anaerobic digesters to make biogas that they use to produce heat. They

a closed loop
クローズドループ、閉ループ

waste stream
廃棄の流れ

pledge to ～
～することを誓約する

organic matter
有機物

amendments
= organic soil
有機土壌改良剤

sludge
汚泥

anaerobic digester
嫌気性消化装置

biogas
バイオガス

convert the remaining solids into a popular soil amendment
30 known as Dillo Dirt. The city makes money selling Dillo Dirt, offsetting some of the cost of treating the wastewater. Instead of composting their waste, as they do in Vancouver, the residents of Austin put food scraps down the drain and through a grinder. The city's industrial-scale harvesters at the wastewater
35 plant do the work of traditional composting but with greater efficiency.

Basically, in order for cities to become sustainable, they will also need to become "Smart Cities." Smart cities will use the latest developments in AI, along with sophisticated algorithms,
40 to monitor infrastructure and optimize sustainability efforts. In this way, cities like Vancouver and Austin can begin to achieve their goal of becoming net-zero producers of waste and pollution, and self-sufficient users of resources like energy and water. Several major urban areas have pledged to become self-
45 sufficient users of energy and water and net-zero producers of waste by becoming "Smart Cities." Achieving those ambitious goals will require a lot of interconnected data.

Smart technology alone will not solve our sustainability issues. It will also require residents of cities to work together,
50 using their imaginations, to find creative solutions. (468 words)

Dillo Dirt
ディロ・ダート（土地改良剤）
offset
埋め合わせをする
compost
〜を堆肥にする

industrial-scale
産業規模の
harvester
ゴミを堆肥に変える装置のこと

net-zero
正味ゼロ

interconnected
相互に接続した

Exercises

A 設問に答えなさい。

1. 次の語句の日本語の意味を答えなさい。

sustainability	crucial	implement	efficiency	optimize

2. In order to create a sustainable city, it is crucial to convert the remaining waste into usable resources. (*l.* 5 ~ *l.*6) を日本語に訳しなさい。

3. Vancouver市が取り組んでいることを日本語で説明しなさい。

4. Austin市が取り組んでいることを日本語で説明しなさい。

B 本文の内容に合うように、質問の答えを選びなさい。

1. What do people need to convert waste into in order to create a sustainable city?

a) Pollution　b) Usable resources　(　　)

c) Organic matter　d) Clean water

2. What was not mentioned as a wasted resource in the article?　(　　)

a) Energy　b) Food　c) Water　d) Oxygen

C 本文の内容と一致しているものにはTを、一致していないものにはFを記入しなさい。

1. (　　) The city of Vancouver produces methane from organic waste and burns it to heat greenhouses.

2. (　　) The city of Austin does not make money selling Dillo Dirt.

3. (　　) The industrial-scale harvesters at the wastewater plant in Austin are more efficient than traditional composting methods.

4. (　　) What is necessary to create sustainable cities is to make them "Smart Cities."
5. (　　) Recycling systems in most cities are 100% efficient at reducing waste at present.
6. (　　) Vancouver and Austin are the only cities that have pledged to become "Smart Cities."

D 各文の空欄に入る語を右から選びなさい。

optimize
achieve
convert
crucial
require

1. The cells absorb light and (　　　　　) it to energy.
2. These pets (　　　　　) some difficult decisions.
3. The new system will (　　　　　) the efficiency with which water is used.
4. This year, our company was able to (　　　　　) all of its production goals.
5. Vitamins are (　　　　　) for maintaining good health.

E 日本語に合うように与えられた語句を並べかえなさい。

He ____.

どれだけ費用がかかっても、彼はその車を買うつもりだ。

to / much / it / that car / how / costs / intends / buy / no matter

F 英文を聞いて、質問の答えをa～cから選び記号で答えなさい。

034
|
036

1. Besides using smart technologies, what do residents of cities need to do to solve their sustainability issues? (　　)
2. Which city has pledged to become the greenest city on earth? (　　)
3. What is the name of the soil amendment produced from the remaining solid waste materials at the wastewater plant in Austin, Texas? (　　)

3RとSDGs

本ユニットの冒頭の3R（スリーアール）について考えてみましょう。日本でも環境省や経済産業省が「3R推進キャンペーン」や「3R政策」を行ってきました。3Rはそれぞれカタカナで「リデュース」「リユース」「リサイクル」ですが具体的にどのようなことを行うのでしょうか。「リデュース」は、日常的に廃棄物の発生を減らすことです。買い物の際にマイバッグを持参するのもこれに属し、3つのRでまずは「リデュース」が重要です。「リユース」は、修理できる機器は修理して使用するなどして繰り返し使うこと、「リサイクル」はアルミ缶や瓶の回収という形で今や日常的になっています。3Rを実行することは、SDGs（Sustainable Development Goals 持続可能な開発目標）—2015年に国連で採択—が目指す持続可能な社会の実現にも関わります。SDGsの17の目標と169のターゲットのうち、3Rはとくにどれに関わるのでしょうか。確認してみてください。

Unit 10

Kombu Will Save the World: Blue Carbon for a Healthier Planet

ブルーカーボンとは？

森林や陸上の植生によって貯蔵される二酸化炭素は「グリーンカーボン」と呼ばれることがありますが、それに対して、最近「ブルーカーボン」という言葉が使われることがあります。その「ブルーカーボン」とは何か、また関連した活動としてどういうものがあるのか、次の英文から読み取ってみましょう。

037

Most people know that planting trees is a good way to reduce the amount of carbon dioxide in the air. However, preserving and creating green space is not the only way to capture carbon from the air. Coastal and marine ecosystems can also play a major role. These ecosystems may include mangrove forests, seagrass meadows, and tidal marshes. They can capture and store a huge amount of carbon. To differentiate them from carbon capture on land, they are referred to as "blue carbon."

Blue carbon ecosystems are five to ten times more effective than rainforests in removing carbon from the air. However, just like forests on land, when seagrasses and mangroves are destroyed, they release carbon back into the atmosphere which contributes to global warming. The problem is that almost one-third of the world's seagrass has been lost in the last 150 years.

In Japan, a network known as Blue Carbon has been formed with the goal to counteract global warming and to "restore the richness" of the sea. Healthy marine ecosystems are important to the world.

Three out of every seven people in the world depend on seafood as their main source of protein and about 44 percent of the world's population lives within 150 kilometers (93 miles) of the ocean. It's quite amazing when you think of the power of algae beds in the sea, that is, places where seaweed and seagrass grow thickly. Not only do they absorb carbon dioxide through the seawater, but they also purify the water quality. In addition, they create a rich environment for fish to spawn. This is vital to the fishing industry and even tourism; the clean and clear sea is

coastal and marine ecosystem 沿岸・海洋生態系

seagrass meadow 海草藻場

tidal marsh 干潟

algae bed 藻場

spawn 産卵する

attractive for activities such as snorkeling and kayaking.

As an island nation, Japan understands the importance of a healthy marine ecosystem. Looking at the website, bluecarbon.jp, one can see a number of initiatives that bring together people from various backgrounds: scientists, fishermen, business leaders, students, and the general public.

One of the projects featured on the blue carbon website is Yokohama based Sachiumi Heroes, directed by Tatsunori Tomimoto. Their idea is to cultivate kelp, also known as kombu, in areas where the seabed has become barren. More kelp in the sea increases the amount of plankton, which feeds creatures and small fish, and in turn attract bigger fish. It is said that kelp can absorb five times as much CO_2 as cedar and can grow four meters in just four months. With the cooperation of local fishermen, Tomimoto has been working to promote kelp farming. Through his project, "the ecosystem will regain circulation, and the environment of the sea will improve," he says.

The city of Yokohama has initiated the Yokohama Blue Carbon Project based on the concept of blue carbon ecosystems advocated by the United Nations. Projects such as the Sachiumi Heroes can be achieved by the participation of not only fishermen but also many people in all parts of society. The continuation of such projects will help make our world a better place to live in for future generations. (511words)

Tatsunori Tomimoto
富本龍徳（幸海ヒーローズ共同代表）

提供：幸海ヒーローズ

barren
不毛の、作物の取れない

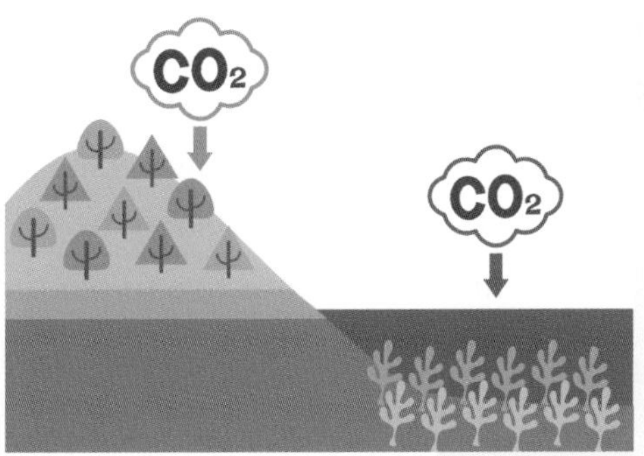

Exercises

A 設問に答えなさい。

1. 次の語句の日本語の意味を答えなさい。

preserve	capture	refer to ～	restore	vital

2. “blue carbon” (*l.* 9) とはどういうものですか。本文に沿って日本語で説明しなさい。

3. Blue carbon ecosystems are five to ten times more effective than rainforests in removing carbon from the air. (*l.* 10～*l.* 11) を日本語に訳しなさい。

4. Sachiumi Heroes (*l.* 36) は、どういう考えを広めようとしていますか。日本語で説明しなさい。

B 本文の内容に合うように、質問の答えを選びなさい。

1. Which one is not an example related to blue carbon? (　　)

a) Mangrove　b) Seagrass　c) Rainforest　d) Tidal marsh

2. Why was the Blue Carbon network set up? (　　)

a) To help make the earth warmer.
b) To help reduce global warming.
c) To reduce the amount of seagrass.
d) To reduce the number of tidal marshes.

C 本文の内容と一致しているものにはＴを、一致していないものにはＦを記入しなさい。

1. (　　) Mangrove forests, seagrass meadows, and tidal marshes are examples of coastal or marine ecosystems.

2. (　　) Rainforests remove five to ten times more carbon from the air than blue carbon ecosystems.

3. (　　) Seagrass absorbs carbon dioxide through seawater.

4. (　　) Wherever there are a lot of seagrasses, there will be fewer fish.
5. (　　) Kelp absorbs five times as much CO_2 as cedar.
6. (　　) Kelp farming improves the environment of the forests.

D 次の各文の空欄に入る語を右から選びなさい。

1. Some people (　　　　) to them as 'gangsters.'
2. She was coming to (　　　　) clean the machine.
3. It's important to (　　　　) between fact and opinion.
4. He was the sort of person you could (　　　　) on.
5. Newspapers (　　　　) a major role in determining how people think about politics.

help
play
depend
refer
differentiate

E 日本語に合うように与えられた語句を並べかえなさい。

Not ____.

彼は、遅れてきたばかりでなく、本も忘れた。

forgot / only / he also / turn up late / he / , / his books / did / but

F 英文を聞いて、英文の後に続くものをa～cから選び記号で答えなさい。

038
|
040

1. Healthy marine ecosystems can (　　　　　).
2. In Japan, the blue carbon network was formed to counteract global warming and to (　　　　　).
3. In order to create a healthy marine environment, people in the Yokohama area are growing (　　　　　).

カーボンニュートラル

日本では政府が2020年に「2050年カーボンニュートラル宣言」を行いました。現在、120以上の国と地域が2050年までに「カーボンニュートラル」が実現される社会を目指しています。カーボンニュートラルとは、温室効果ガス（CO_2、N_2O、フロンガスなど）について、排出量から吸収量と除去量を差し引いた合計をゼロにすることです。差し引きをゼロにすることがここでいう「ニュートラル」ということになります。本ユニットで扱われた「ブルーカーボン」は吸収や除去に関わることになりますが、それだけでなく、「排出量」自体を減らすことができれば、カーボンニュートラルの実現に近づきます。環境省は（「脱炭素ポータル」https://ondankataisaku.env.go.jp/carbon_neutral/about/）、2025年までに重点対策を行って、2030年には「脱炭素ドミノ」を伝播させる方針を打ち出しています。

Is This Your Last Textbook?

ChatGPTの教育に対する影響について

2022年11月にOpenAIという企業が公開したChatGPTは、高度で多機能な技術のため、大きな注目を集めているようです。ChatGPTとはどのようなものか、また、特に教育における影響や、注意すべき点などについて、次の英文から読み取ってみましょう。

041

Even before the debut of OpenAI's ChatGPT, you were probably already familiar with chatbots. At the beginning of 2023, instructors all over the world were both excited and terrified by the introduction of ChatGPT. Simple chatbots have been used for years in customer service to simulate real conversation. For example, if you need help setting up your Wi-Fi router, you can call the company and talk to a live person, or you can interact by text with an AI chatbot on the company's website.

OpenAI
アメリカの起業家・投資家が集まって2015年に設立された人工知能（AI）の研究機関

ChatGPT is the most powerful AI chatbot yet. It reacts naturally, like a personal assistant. If you search Google or other search engines for a broccoli recipe, you must sort through a list of many websites. Ask ChatGPT for a broccoli recipe, and you will immediately be given step-by-step instructions:

yet
（最上級の後に用いて）これまでで最も～な

Human (H): Do you have any lunch recipe ideas that use broccoli?
ChatGPT (C): Yes, I have a few lunch recipe ideas that use broccoli. Here are three options: (three recipes follow)
H: For the first recipe, I don't have bacon, sunflower seeds, or red onion.
C: No problem! You can still make a delicious broccoli salad without those ingredients. Here's a simplified version of the recipe using just a few basic ingredients: (recipe follows)

Clearly, ChatGPT is handy in helping with recipe ideas, but what about its impact on education? Why not ask ChatGPT?

H: In 75 words or less, can you tell me the implications of ChatGPT on education?
C: As a large language model, ChatGPT has the potential to transform

education by providing instant access to vast amounts of knowledge and information. It can assist students in researching, answering questions, and providing explanations on a wide range of topics. ChatGPT can also provide personalized learning experiences by adapting to the individual needs and preferences of students. However, it is important to note that ChatGPT is not a replacement for teachers or traditional learning methods but can be a useful tool to enhance and supplement learning.

Like the calculator or electronic dictionary, ChatGPT is another tool, but one that is expected to have a much more significant impact on various aspects of life including education. Some teachers are worried that students will submit essays produced by ChatGPT in only a few seconds. OpenAI has already provided an AI text classifier to help identify whether text is human-written or AI-generated.

As this new era begins, many language teachers are considering how it will affect their classes. The possibilities are endless. A teacher can instruct ChatGPT to generate exercise questions for any text, including this one. It's a huge time saver for busy teachers. One concern is that language teachers will become obsolete. If you are motivated, you can learn a language on your own. In the evolution of language learning, people have benefited from books, records, tapes, CDs, smartphone apps, and now the revolutionary ChatGPT. One of the most powerful motivators, however, has not changed: human contact. Fancy tools come and go, but nothing beats a real human staring you down to get you to speak up. (506 words)

obsolete
時代遅れの、必要とされなくなった

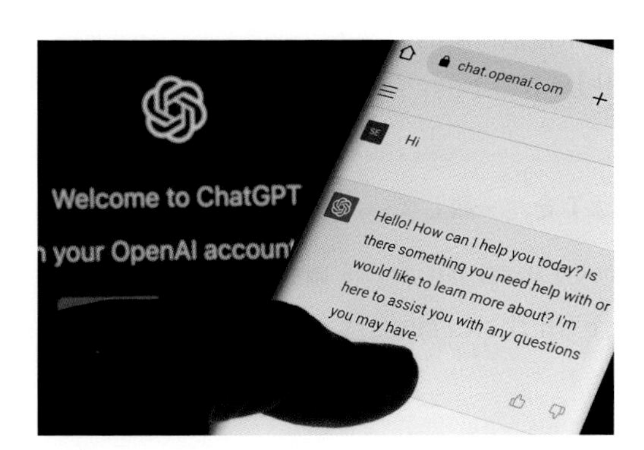

Exercises

A 設問に答えなさい。

1. 次の語句の日本語の意味を答えなさい。

terrified	implication	supplement (*v.*)	evolution	beat

2. 本文において、ChatGPT に教育に対する影響を尋ねた際に ChatGPT が回答したことで、重要だと述べていることはどういうことですか。日本語で説明しなさい。

3. 本文において、語学教師が考えている授業への影響はどういうことですか。日本語で説明しなさい。

4. One of the most powerful motivators, however, has not changed: human contact. Fancy tools come and go, but nothing beats a real human staring you down to get you to speak up. (*l.* 55 ~ *l.* 58) を日本語に訳しなさい。

B 本文の内容に合うように、質問の答えを選びなさい。

1. What can ChatGPT do if you ask for a broccoli recipe? (　　)

a) It can provide a list of websites to search through.
b) It can give you step-by-step instructions immediately.
c) It can't help you with recipes.
d) It will ask you for more information before providing a recipe.

2. What is the concern regarding ChatGPT and language teachers? (　　)

a) That language teachers will become obsolete.
b) That language teachers will become more effective.
c) That language teachers will not be motivated.
d) That language teachers will be too busy to use ChatGPT.

C 本文の内容と一致しているものには T を、一致していないものには F を記入しなさい。

1. (　　) Simple chatbots have been used for years in customer service.

2. (　　) The author did not have all the necessary ingredients for one of the recipes.

3. (　　) ChatGPT is not a replacement for teachers.
4. (　　) ChatGPT provides instant access to limited amounts of knowledge and information.
5. (　　) Human contact is no longer important in language learning.
6. (　　) ChatGPT can write essays in only a few seconds.

D 次の各文の空欄に入る語を右から選びなさい。

evolution
own
impact
potential
access

1. The stress of her job is having a negative (　　　　) on her health.
2. All public buildings should provide wheelchair (　　　　).
3. The disease has the (　　　　) to cause a global health emergency.
4. He did it on his (　　　　).
5. We have been able to watch her (　　　　) into a world-class runner.

E 日本語に合うように与えられた語句を並べかえなさい。文頭に来るべき語も小文字になっています。

____.

物事がいかに早く変化したかに気付くのはおもしろい。

changed / things / note / is / have / quickly / interesting / it / how / to

F 英文を聞いて、質問の答えを a ～ c から選び記号で答えなさい。

042
|
044

1. How is ChatGPT different from simple chatbots? (　　)
2. What is the main function of ChatGPT in education? (　　)
3. What is the biggest motivator in language learning? (　　)

教育との関係

ChatGPT は外国語の習得に関して、従来のツールよりも楽しく効率的に学習できそうですし、その他にも利点の多いものですね。その一方で、高等教育機関においてオンラインでレポートを提出することも増えている今日、本文にもあるように、学生が ChatGPT で作成した文書をレポートとして提出することになったら…、という懸念が出ています。人間が書いたものなのか、AI によって書かれたものかを AI で識別できるとしても、将来的には、どちらの文章なのかを判別できないほどの文章を AI が作成できるようになる可能性も否定できません。結局のところ、この技術がさらに進展すると、AI 作成によるレポート提出への対策として、オンラインでのレポート提出の機会が減って、対面での論述筆記試験という昔ながらのやり方が増えることも考えられます。新技術の発展に伴い、教育の現場ではレポートや論文作成に関わる倫理教育の重要性がこれまで以上に増していくでしょう。

Unit 12

Astro Boy and the DART Mission

鉄腕アトムとNASAのDARTミッションについて

探査機による衝突によって小惑星の軌道を変え、小惑星の地球衝突を回避するための実験がNASAによって行われています。鉄腕アトムが地球を守るために取った行動とどことなく重なっていることが現実になってきているようです。次の英文から内容を読み取ってみましょう。

045

"Astro Boy" is a sci-fi masterpiece created by Osamu Tezuka. For those of you not familiar with the character, the boy robot uses nuclear power to propel himself, and he has human-like emotions. From 1963 to 1966, it was broadcast on TV as Japan's first domestically-produced animated series. The last episode, which aired on New Year's Eve in 1966, is very sad, but moving. As Earth's last chance to avoid destruction, Astro Boy guides a rocket into the sun to suppress its deadly rays. The "DART" mission reminds us of that last episode of Astro Boy. Although the animation was not based on reality, if the technology used in the DART mission had been available at that time, Astro Boy wouldn't have had to sacrifice his life by plunging into the sun.

While it has been established that the sun should remain stable for several billions of years into the future, there is a real threat that an asteroid could impact Earth in the much nearer future, which has the potential of being an extinction level event for humanity. As a result of this concern, NASA developed a mission called DART (Double Asteroid Redirection Test) to see if it would be possible to alter the course of an asteroid with a kinetic impact millions of kilometers before it could potentially reach Earth. On November 24, 2021, the DART spacecraft was successfully launched from Vandenberg Space Force Base in California on a SpaceX Falcon 9 rocket. It should be noted that this mission was a test of technology, and that the target asteroid was not a potential threat to Earth.

The initial stage of the mission concluded on September 26, 2022, with a head-on collision of the DART spacecraft with the

propel 前に押し出す、進ませる

domestically-produced 国産の

kinetic 動的な

Vandenberg Space Force Base ヴァンデンバーグ宇宙軍基地

a SpaceX Falcon 9 rocket SpaceX社が開発したファルコン9ロケット

a head-on collision 正面衝突

target asteroid Dimorphos (diameter: 160 meters), which is a smaller moonlet asteroid revolving around the larger asteroid Didymos (diameter: 780 meters). Didymos means "twin" in Greek, which explains the word "double" in the mission's name. The objective of a head-on impact was to slow the transit of Dimorphos around Didymos, thereby allowing gravity to gradually pull the two bodies closer to each other. It was determined that lowering the orbit in this way would most likely assure that Dimorphos would not fly off in a random direction, possibly towards Earth.

Dimorphos ディモルフォス

Didymos ディディモス

lower the orbit 軌道を下げる（ディディモスを周回する軌道の距離が短くなること）

After analysis of data obtained from the first two weeks of both space and ground-based observations, it was estimated that the asteroid's transit was shortened by about 32 minutes, which resulted in a fairly substantial change in the orbit of Dimorphos around Didymos. This was clearly a resounding achievement for the tiny spacecraft, as mission success was initially determined to be a change of 73 seconds, or more.

In the future, we should be able to alter the course of a rogue asteroid in our solar system to deflect it in any direction we desire long before it could be a danger to Earth. Just as Astro Boy was able to save Earth from certain doom, there is now hope that one day we can save Earth from the impact of a potentially life-ending asteroid thanks to the DART mission.

(520 words)

rogue 軌道から外れた

deflect そらす

doom 破滅

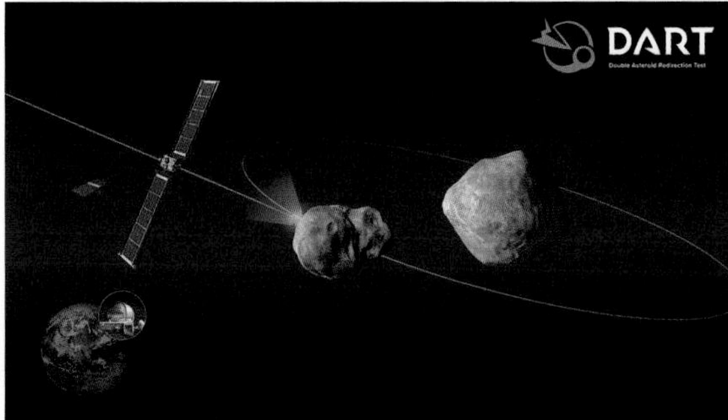

©NASA

© 手塚プロダクション

Exercises

A 設問に答えなさい。

1. 次の語句の日本語の意味を答えなさい。

sacrifice (*v.*)	asteroid	impact (*n./v.*)	alter	launch (*v.*)

2. Although the animation was not based on reality, if the technology used in the DART mission had been available at that time, Astro Boy wouldn't have had to sacrifice his life by plunging into the sun. (*l.10*～*l.13*) を日本語に訳しなさい。

3. a real threat (*l.15*～*l.16*) とありますが、どういった脅威ですか。日本語で答えなさい。

4. the objective of a head-on impact (*l.33*) とありますが、どういった目的ですか。日本語で答えなさい。

B 本文の内容に合うように、質問の答えを選びなさい。

1. Why did Astro Boy guide a rocket into the sun? (　　)

a) To move it farther away from Earth.
b) To move it closer to Earth.
c) To slow it down.
d) To suppress its deadly rays.

2. Why did NASA develop the DART mission? (　　)

a) To see if they could destroy an asteroid.
b) To see if it would be possible to alter the course of an asteroid.
c) To see if they could make an asteroid impact Earth.
d) To see if they could suppress the rays of the sun.

C 本文の内容と一致しているものにはＴを、一致していないものにはＦを記入しなさい。

1. (　　) The objective of a head-on impact was to speed up the transit of Dimorphos around Didymos.

2. (　　) NASA analyzed data obtained from both space and ground-based observations.

3. (　　) Lowering the orbit of Dimorphos around Didymos would most likely prevent the moonlet asteroid from flying off in a random direction.
4. (　　) Dimorphos is larger than Didymos.
5. (　　) Astro Boy is based on reality.
6. (　　) NASA observed a substantial change in the orbit of Dimorphos around Didymos after the impact of the DART spacecraft.

D 各文の空欄に入る語を右から選びなさい。

1. Alcohol can (　　　　　) a person's mood.
2. Your hair and eyes (　　　　　) me of your mother.
3. The interview will (　　　　　) tomorrow.
4. Police (　　　　　) the crowd at 30,000.
5. By staying at home, he manages to (　　　　　) all contact with strangers.

remind
avoid
estimate
alter
air

E 日本語に合うように与えられた語句を並べかえなさい。

She ____.

彼女は、転ばなければ、そのレースに勝っていただろう。

she / the race / tripped / if / have / would / hadn't / won

F 英文を聞いて、質問の答えを a ～ c から選び記号で答えなさい。

046–048

1. How many minutes was the orbit of Dimorphos around Didymos shortened after two weeks of observations? (　　)
2. When was the final episode of Astro Boy aired on TV in Japan? (　　)
3. When did the DART spacecraft impact Didymos? (　　)

地球を守る

小惑星が地球に衝突して地球が破壊されるのを防ぐという話から、映画『アルマゲドン』を思い出された方もあるでしょう。「地球を守る」ということを人間はいつ頃から現実に意識するようになったのでしょうか。本ユニットの冒頭にあるように、鉄腕アトムは「地球を守る」行動を実行しました。作者の手塚治虫はどういう思いでこの **"The last episode"** (*l.*5～*l.*6) を書いたのかを考えさせられます。手塚のアニメは、他の作品の場合も単に読んで面白いかどうかだけではなく、どんなメッセージがそこに込められているのかをよく考えて読むとよいでしょう。現在、地球上では相変わらず戦争や紛争が生じています。地球全体で取り組まなければならない課題には、気候変動や食料問題、感染症や人口問題など実に多くのことがあり、戦争などしている場合ではないと感じる方は多いと思います。「地球を守る」という考え方は、今後、いっそう重要になっていくはずです。

Unit 13

Perceptions of Colors

色の認識について

「虹の色は何色か」と聞かれて、日本人は「７色」と答えると思いますが、文化によって虹の色の数は異なることが知られています。次の色に関する英文を読み、内容を読み取ってみましょう。

049

There are about 50 different ways to describe snow in several Inuit and Yupik languages, while some languages around the world only have one word to describe it. Snow is a very important part of Inuit and Yupik life, but for many people living in Africa, it is just something they have seen in pictures, a movie, or on TV. Regardless of how many ways a particular culture describes the concept of snow, they all use a term that means the color "white" when describing what it looks like.

Indeed, the World Color Survey, which collected data on color terminology from pre-industrial societies, determined that all of the 110 languages they studied have a word for the basic colors of black and white. Many languages also include words that mean red, yellow, green and blue. More color-complex languages also include terms for orange, purple, pink, gray, and brown. Although the survey discovered an elaborate assortment of terms used for different shades of colors in each language, it proposed that there is an underlying universal, biological aspect to the way humans describe the basic colors.

Even though many scholars disagree with this hypothesis, there is no question that individual cultures, and even individuals within those cultures, use the language of color to interpret the world around them. A dynamic process takes place in which language informs culture and culture informs language, both evolving to meet the needs of the members of society. People growing up in a specific culture learn the complex meanings pertaining to colors in their culture. There are clearly-defined semantic rules that are internalized from a very early age, but problems can arise when these meanings are

Yupik
ユピック族（シベリアおよびアラスカ南西部に住む民族）

the World Color Survey
世界色彩語彙調査
terminology
専門用語、術語
pre-industrial societies
ここでは書き言葉のない社会のことを意味している

pertain to～
～に関係がある

exported to other cultures.

30 For example, in the 1950s, PepsiCo changed the color of their vending machines in Southeast Asia from dark blue to a lighter shade of blue they thought would be more appealing to their customers in the relatively hot and humid climate of that area of the world. What they did not realize is that to 35 Southeast Asians, the hue of blue they used is the color associated with death and sorrow, and not the energizing and refreshing image they thought it represented. They became aware of the issue only after they noticed a significant drop in sales.

PepsiCo は現在の社名。当時の社名は the Pepsi-Cola Company。

hue
色相、色彩
energizing
エネルギーを与える

40 In fact, colors have a wide variety of meanings, depending on the culture. Sometimes, these meanings are exact opposites. For example, in North America, the color red is associated with danger, while in Asia it is associated with happiness. In China, for example, if children receive a red envelope full of money 45 from their parents or grandparents at New Year's, they experience the positive feelings pertaining to the color red. On the other hand, in the United States, "seeing red" means that someone is so angry that they literally see red! (471 words)

see red
かっとなる（牛が赤い布を見て興奮することからきている）

	Western / America	Asia	Middle East	Latin America
Red	Danger Love Passion	Happiness Joy Celebration	Danger Caution Evil	Fire Religion Passion
Yellow	Happiness Warmth Caution	Sacred Royalty Courage	Happiness Strength Mourning	Death Sorrow Mourning
Blue	Trust Authority Masculinity	Immortality Strength Femininity	Protection Holiness Spirituality	Trust Religion Serenity
Green	Nature Luck Greed	Nature Youth Infidelity	Strength Luck Fertility	Nature Death Danger
Purple	Wealth Royalty Fame	Wealth Nobility Mourning	Wealth Virtue Omen	Death Sorrow Mourning

Source: https://summalinguae.com/language-culture/colurs-across-cultures/

Exercises

A **設問に答えなさい。**

1. 次の語句の日本語の意味を答えなさい。

regardless of ～	concept	term	determine	be associated with ～

2. Although the survey discovered an elaborate assortment of terms used for different shades of colors in each language, it proposed that there is an underlying universal, biological aspect to the way humans describe the basic colors. (*l.15*～*l.18*) を日本語に訳しなさい。

3. 本文中にあるペプシコの例は、どういう事例ですか。日本語で具体的に説明しなさい。

4. 最後のパラグラフに述べてある red という色に関する北アメリカとアジアでの意味合いの違いについて日本語で説明しなさい。

B **本文の内容に合うように、質問の答えを選びなさい。**

1. According to the article, what color would not be considered a basic color?
a) Black　b) White　c) Indigo　d) Red　(　　)

2. What is the color red associated with in North America?　(　　)
a) Danger　b) Death　c) Sorrow　d) Happiness

C **本文の内容と一致しているものにはTを、一致していないものにはFを記入しなさい。**

1. (　　) The World Color Survey determined that some of the languages they studied did not have words for the basic colors of black and white.

2. (　　) People growing up in a specific culture learn the complex meanings pertaining to colors in their culture.

3. (　　) The hue of blue PepsiCo used for the color on their vending machines in Southeast Asia is associated with refreshment and energization for the people living there.

4. ( ) Sometimes, a color can have the exact opposite meaning in two different cultures.
5. ( ) The Inuit and Yupik have only one way to describe snow in their languages.
6. ( ) The World Color Survey proposed that there is an underlying universal, biological aspect to the way humans describe basic colors.

D 各文の空欄に入る語を右から選びなさい。

1. There is a similar word in many languages, (   ) in French and Italian.
2. I hate (   ) she always criticizes me.
3. The law requires equal treatment for all, (   ) race, religion, or sex.
4. Schools in the north tend to be better equipped, (   ) those in the south are relatively poor.
5. The expenses you claim can vary enormously, (   ) travel distances involved.

depending on
while
regardless of
for example
the way

E 日本語に合うように与えられた語句を並べかえなさい。

What ______________________________.

私を怒らせたのは、彼のあなたに対する扱いである。

angry / how / he / me / you / made / treated / was

F 英文を聞いて、質問の答えをa〜cから選び記号で答えなさい。

050–052

1. What is the color red associated with in Asia? ( )
2. From how many different languages did the World Color Survey collect data? ( )
3. What color do some cultures not have a term for? ( )

リンゴは本当に「赤色」なのか

カント(1724-1804)という哲学者は、「現象」と「物自体」を区別して、わたしたちが認識できるのは現象であって、物自体ではないとしました。現象とは、わたしたちに現れている側面のことで、リンゴは「赤色」としてわたしたちには現れています。しかし、決してリンゴというものそのものを、つまり「物自体」を認識しているのではないというのです。ところで、猫は目の構造上「赤色」を認識できないとされています。猫には赤色は「灰色」とか「黄色」に見えるそうですが、この場合も、猫は物自体ではなく、「灰色」「黄色」という現象を認識していることになります。人間同士の場合、言語はそれぞれ異なっていても、ものは同じ仕方で人間の感覚を刺激することから、思考のレベルでは一致するように感じられますが、本文にあるように、何かを「見る」ということでさえ、それぞれの言語の色の区分からの影響があり、それゆえ思考法が同じであるとは限りません。

Unit 14

Jumping to Conclusions

結論に飛びつく私たちの認知の特性について

私たちの多くは、結論に飛びつくという特性があるようです。どういうことが原因で結論に飛びつくのか、また、それを回避するにはどういう手段があるのか、次の英文から読み取ってみましょう。

053

Jumping to conclusions is a term used to describe when people make decisions regarding situations without taking into consideration all of the facts involved. This often leads to conclusions that are misleading or untrue. For example, someone might come to the conclusion that a person they like is ghosting them on social media because they don't respond to their messages, when in fact the person accused of ghosting may just have lost or misplaced their smartphone.

ghost
急に連絡をしなくなる

People jump to conclusions all of the time, even though doing so can lead to a variety of issues, some of which can have serious consequences. For example, Jerome Groopman, author of *How Doctors Think*, says that "most incorrect diagnoses are due to physicians' misconceptions of their patients, not technical mistakes like a faulty lab test." These misconceptions are often the result of preconceived notions physicians have regarding their patients based on age, sex, or ethnicity. There are many examples where physicians jumped to conclusions that caused more harm than good in the treatment of their patients.

Jerome Groopman (1952-)
ジェローム・グループマン（ハーバード大学医学部教授、多くの新聞や科学雑誌に寄稿するなど執筆活動も行っている）

Researchers have identified several common ways people jump to conclusions.

- **Casual assumption.** This involves making assumptions based on previous knowledge, experience, or beliefs. For example, seeing a restaurant with a shabby exterior and immediately deciding that the food they serve must not be good.
- **Fortune-telling.** This involves assuming that you can predict what will happen in certain situations in the future. For

casual
不用意な、思い付きの
shabby
みすぼらしい
fortune-telling
認知科学の分野では、この用語は、一般的な「占い」とは違って、実際の可能性を考えることなく未来のことを（悪く）予想することに対して使われることがある。

example, thinking that failing an English test is inevitable no matter how much you prepare, so you don't even bother to study for it.

- **Mind reading.** This involves assuming that you can tell what other people are thinking without any evidence to back up this assumption. For example, thinking that your boss doesn't like you just because he didn't smile when you greeted him, and you wonder what you did wrong.
- **Labeling.** This involves making generalizations about people based on stereotypes associated with a religious, political, racial, gender, or age group they are a part of. For example, assuming that all old people are bad drivers.

Jumping to conclusions is not necessarily a bad thing to do. After all, our cognitive system relies on mental shortcuts, which are often called "rules of thumb" or "educated guesses," to increase the speed of our judgment and decision-making processes in our daily lives. Often times, the conclusions we arrive at appear to be correct, but, unfortunately, many times they can also be wrong.

The main way to avoid jumping to conclusions is to make sure to use a valid, evidence-based reasoning process to come to conclusions, instead of relying on intuitive judgments that are based on insufficient data. It is a good idea to slow down, collect all of the facts, and then come to a conclusion based on those facts and not just your gut instinct. Doing so could drastically reduce the number of awkward social situations you experience in your life. (485 words)

cognitive system 認知体系
rules of thumb 経験則
educated guess 知識・経験に基づく推測
gut instinct 本能的直感

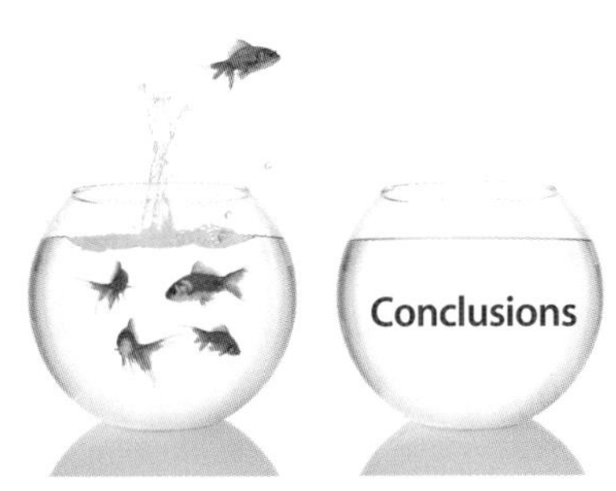

Exercises

A **設問に答えなさい。**

1. 次の語句の日本語の意味を答えなさい。

accuse	diagnosis	misconception	predict	assumption

2. “jumping to conclusions” (*l.* 1) とはどういう時に使われる用語ですか。本文に沿って日本語で説明しなさい。

3. 本文に述べてある研究者が特定した「結論に飛びつく」やり方の４つについて、見出しとなっている語句を日本語に直しなさい。

・	・
・	・

4. The main way to avoid jumping to conclusions is to make sure to use a valid, evidence-based reasoning process to come to conclusions, instead of relying on intuitive judgments that are based on insufficient data. (*l.* 49～*l.* 52) を日本語に訳しなさい。

B **本文の内容に合うように、質問の答えを選びなさい。**

1. Which common way people jump to conclusions is associated with predicting the future? (　　)

a) Mind reading　b) Labeling　c) Fortune-telling　d) Casual assumption

2. What is one way to avoid jumping to conclusions? (　　)

a) Use a rule of thumb.　b) Collect all of the facts.
c) Make an educated guess.　d) Rely on gut instinct.

C **本文の内容と一致しているものにはＴを、一致していないものにはＦを記入しなさい。**

1. (　　) Casual assumptions involve making assumptions based on previous knowledge, experience, or beliefs.

2. (　　) Making the assumption that all old people are bad drivers is an example of mind reading.

3. (　　) People often jump to conclusions.

4. (　　) Jerome Groopman claims that most incorrect diagnoses by doctors is the result of faulty lab tests.
5. (　　) Jumping to conclusions is always a bad thing to do.
6. (　　) We rely on rules of thumb and educated guesses to increase the speed of our judgment and decision-making processes.

D 次の各文の空欄に入る語を右から選びなさい。

1. He thinks the treatment may (　　　　) more harm than good.
2. It is almost impossible for the average person to (　　　　) an informed decision.
3. We will (　　　　) your recent illness into consideration when grading your exams.
4. We need to (　　　　) the causes of unemployment.
5. You can't (　　　　) him of being rude: he's always extremely polite.

accuse
take
identify
make
cause

E 日本語に合うように与えられた語句を並べかえなさい。文頭に来るべき語も小文字になっています。

____.

新しい証拠によって、私たちは間違っているという結論に繋がるかもしれない。

that / we / new evidence / are / lead to / might / wrong / the conclusion

F 英文を聞いて、質問の答えをa～cから選び記号で答えなさい。

054–056

1. What is not a way to avoid jumping to conclusions? (　　)
2. Which common way of jumping to conclusions involves making generalizations based on stereotypes? (　　)
3. What is not considered to be a mental shortcut used to increase the speed of our judgement and decision-making processes? (　　)

クリティカルシンキング

長い説明や発言を聞いていて、先に結論を言ってほしいと感じることがあるかもしれません。一方、結論を急いで拙速な判断を行って失敗することもあります。とくに若い人にとっては、まず論理的に吟味する力を身につけることが大切だと思います。Aという主張（結論）に賛成の人と反対の人がいて議論しているときに、あなたがどちらに賛成するかは、結論Aに賛成する「理由」と、Aに反対する「理由」のどちらが説得的であるかによるでしょう。ここでお勧めしたいのは、クリティカルシンキング（Critical Thinking）です。クリティカルシンキングは、訳せば「批判的思考」ですが、この「批判的」というのは誰かをやたらと批判することではなく、ある主張の内容を鵜呑みにすることなく、まず論理的に吟味すること、最終的にそれを受け入れるのであれ拒否するのであれ、まず丹念に吟味する思考です。その手法はいろいろありますので、関連の書籍などで調べてみてください。

Unit 15

Information Overload

情報のオーバーロードに対する対策

現代社会は情報にあふれていて、過剰な状況とも言えそうです。このような状況ではどのような問題が起こりうるのか次の英文から読み取ってみましょう。

057

Do you sometimes feel overwhelmed by all of the information that is coming to you constantly from your electronic devices? Do you often find yourself distracted by push updates from your favorite newsfeed or online chat app? At the end of the day, do you often feel that you haven't accomplished anything, yet you are exhausted? Well, you are not alone. With information technology at our fingertips 24 hours a day, millions of people feel this way, and a lot of it has to do with something known as "information overload."

Information overload describes the excess of information available to a person aiming to complete a task or make a decision. This disrupts our decision-making process, resulting in poor, or even no decisions being made. The term was coined by Bertram Gross, professor of political science, in his 1964 work, *The Managing of Organizations*. Information overload has been a problem throughout history, particularly during the Renaissance and Industrial Revolution periods. However, the advent of the Information Age, with constant access to powerful and low-cost data collection on an automated basis, has brought us more information than we can often make sense of.

As a result, many people may experience stress, which was described as "information anxiety" by Richard Saul Wurman. He argued that information anxiety isn't caused by the large amount of information in itself, but rather by the large amount of irrelevant information. Much of the information we receive is often biased, misleading, or simply not true. "Analysis paralysis" is the term used to describe the inability to make decisions based on the overwhelming amount of extraneous

newsfeed
配信されるオンラインニュース

Bertram (Myron) Gross (1912-1997)
バートラム・グロス（アメリカの政治学・社会学者）

advent
出現、到来

the Information Age
情報化時代

information anxiety
情報不安症

Richard Saul Wurman (1935-)
リチャード・ソール・ワーマン（アメリカの建築家・グラフィックデザイナー、TEDの創設者）

analysis paralysis
分析まひ

extraneous
外部からの、無関係の

information we are constantly exposed to.

30 Researchers have identified six key consequences of information overload:

1. Poor decision-making
2. Memory loss
3. Stress and anxiety
4. Low productivity
5. Short attention span
6. Lack of self-confidence

Fortunately, there are a few things you can do to mitigate these symptoms.

mitigate ～を軽減する

40 First of all, you should write down your thoughts and goals. Write everything that is bothering you in a journal. You will realize that they are not that significant at all once you look at them objectively. You should also make a list of your goals for each day, prioritizing the activities that will lead to achieving those goals.

The second thing you should do is remove nonproductive apps and websites from your smartphone, tablet, or home computer. Most of the useless and misleading information we receive comes from the Internet. Many people spend hours every day scrolling through their feeds and checking their notifications. These constant distractions prevent us from staying focused on our goals.

feed = newsfeed

If the tips mentioned above do not seem to help, you can always do a "digital detox." You simply stop using your electronic devices for anything other than work or school-related activities for a week. An information cleanse can benefit your psychological well-being. It would give you time to rediscover an old hobby you had a passion for years ago, or, perhaps, you could find a new activity to pursue that doesn't have anything to do with your electronic devices. The choice is yours to make.

digital detox デジタル・デトックス（デジタル機器を一定期間使わないこと）

(519 words)

Exercises

A 設問に答えなさい。

1. 次の語句の日本語の意味を答えなさい。

overload (*n.*)	overwhelm (*v.*)	irrelevant	misleading	symptom

2. With information technology at our fingertips 24 hours a day, millions of people feel this way, and a lot of it has to do with something known as "information overload." (*l.* 6 ~ *l.*9) を日本語に訳しなさい。

3. six key consequences of information overload (*l.* 30 ~ *l.*31) を具体的に６つ日本語で答えなさい。

·	·	·
·	·	·

4. there are a few things you can do to mitigate these symptoms (*l.* 38 ~ *l.*39) とありますが、３つに分けて、日本語でできるだけ簡潔にまとめなさい。

·

·

·

B 本文の内容に合うように、質問の答えを選びなさい。

1. What has not been identified as a key consequence of information overload?

a) Poor decision-making　　b) Low productivity　　(　　)
c) Lack of self-confidence　　d) Sleepless nights

2. What is the specific term used to describe the inability to make decisions based on the overwhelming amount of irrelevant information we are exposed to?

a) Information anxiety　　b) Information overload　　(　　)
c) Analysis paralysis　　d) Stress

C 本文の内容と一致しているものにはＴを、一致していないものにはＦを記入しなさい。

1. (　　) Information overload describes the excess of information available to a person aiming to complete a task or make a decision.

2. (　　) Writing down everything that is bothering you is one way to mitigate the symptoms of information overload.

3. (　　) Information anxiety is only caused by the large amount of information we are exposed to.
4. (　　) Memory loss has been identified as one of the key consequences of information overload.
5. (　　) Most of the useless and misleading information we receive comes from watching television.
6. (　　) Information overload has only been a problem since the beginning of the Information Age.

D 各文の空欄に入る語を右から選びなさい。

1. His back injury may (　　　　) him from playing in tomorrow's game.
2. Engineers (　　　　) much time and energy developing brilliant solutions.
3. Were you able to (　　　　) sense of what he said?
4. Fifty percent of road accidents (　　　　) in head injuries.
5. This question doesn't have anything to (　　　　) with the main topic of the survey.

do
prevent
result
make
spend

E 日本語に合うように与えられた語句を並べかえなさい。

Don't ______________________________.

ポケットに手を入れて立ってはいけません。

in / your pockets / stand / with / your hands

058–060

F 英文を聞いて、質問の答えをａ～ｃから選び記号で答えなさい。

1. Who coined the term "information overload?" (　　)
2. What does an "information cleanse" refer to? (　　)
3. What period in history was not mentioned in the article? (　　)

情報リテラシー information literacy

情報のオーバーロードに対する対策として、現代社会において必要とされている能力である情報リテラシーを身につけることも大切です。あのことはどこで調べればよいのだろう？と思ったとき、情報が多すぎて必要な情報にたどりつけないと困ります。何をどのように調べればよいのかということは、まさに情報リテラシーの問題です。またそれは、どの情報を信用すればよいのかということにも関わります。何か大惨事が起こったとき、みなさんはブログやツイッター、調査機関の報告書、著名人の発言、政府の発表のどれを信用するでしょうか。フェイクニュースや意図的な情報操作によって判断を誤ることがないように注意が必要です。本ユニットにでてくる、疲労しないように情報収集の仕事を行うということも、情報リテラシーを身につけることで改善できることもあるでしょう。

References

Unit 1 **Getting to the Roots of Meaning**
Roberts, Wesley / Janine Landowski, "Epidemiology 101, Endemics, pandemics and epidemics, explained," Baptist Health. (May 31, 2022)
https://www.baptistjax.com/juice/stories/covid-19/epidemiology-101

Unit 2 **Cool Ideas ...**
「熱さまシリーズについて」小林製薬株式会社
https://www.kobayashi.co.jp/brand/netsusama/products/episode.html

Unit 3 **Happy Anniversary Snoopy: 50+ years of NASA and Peanuts Collaboration**
"Snoopy to Fly on NASA's Artemis I Moon Mission", NASA, Nov 13, 2021.
https://www.nasa.gov/feature/snoopy-to-fly-on-nasas-artemis-i-moon-mission

Unit 4 **Sweat the Details**
Sato, Masaya, "Sweat pores improve fingerprint recognition tenfold, researchers say," NIKKEI Asia, May 1, 2018.
https://asia.nikkei.com/Business/Technology/Sweat-pores-improve-fingerprint-recognition-tenfold-researchers-say

Unit 5 **The Legacy of the *Rikejo***
"Rikejo: Japan's Pioneering Women in Science," Tokyo Institute of Technology, June 2014.
https://www.titech.ac.jp/english/public-relations/about/stories/research-pioneer-rikejo

Unit 6 **Rubik's Cube**
Kennedy, Mark, "The mind behind the Rubik's Cube celebrates a lasting puzzle," AP News, December 2, 2022.
https://apnews.com/article/rubiks-cube-inventor-10e05bf5c9e27c0cc6700c9dfb486e35

Unit 7 **From Field to Fabulous: The Evolution of Kanazawa Station**
「鉄道開業 150年　私たちは、駅をめざして旅に出る」井土聡子、日本経済新聞 2022年10月9日 The Style 11面
https://www.nikkei.com/article/DGXZQOUD163VR0W2A910C2000000/
(2022年10月14日)
The History of Kanazawa Station
https://www.kanazawastation.com/the-history-of-kanazawa-station/

Unit 8 **Zoom Fatigue**
Machemer, Theresa, "'Zoom fatigue' may be with us for years. Here's how we'll cope," *National Geographic*, 20 April 2021.
https://www.nationalgeographic.co.uk/science-and-technology/2021/04/zoom-fatigue-may-be-with-us-for-years-heres-how-well-cope

Unit 9 **Creating** Sustainable Cities
Webber, Michael E. "Sustainable Cities Put Waste to Work-Transforming costly wastes into valuable resources can make cities highly efficient," *Scientific American*, July 1, 2017.
https://www.scientificamerican.com/article/sustainable-cities-put-waste-to-work/

Unit 10 Kombu Will Save the World: Blue Carbon for a Healthier Planet
「幸海（さちうみ）ヒーローズ」HP
https://sachiumi.com/

Unit 11 Is This Your Last Textbook?
OpenAI. "ChatGPT: A large language model." Accessed on February 27th, 2023.

Unit 12 Astro Boy and the DART Mission
"Double Asteroid Redirection Test," The Johns Hopkins University Applied Physics Laboratory.
https://dart.jhuapl.edu/Mission/index.php
"NASA Confirms DART Mission Impact Changed Asteroid's Motion in Space"
https://www.nasa.gov/press-release/nasa-confirms-dart-mission-impact-changed-asteroid-s-motion-in-space

Unit 13 Perceptions of Colors
"Colors Across Cultures: A Color Psychology Guide for Brands," Summa Linguae, October 27, 2021.
https://summalinguae.com/language-culture/colours-across-cultures/
Jones, Nicola, "Over the Rainbow: How Culture Shapes Color," Atmos, November 1, 2022
https://atmos.earth/over-the-rainbow-color-perception-science/
Lindsey, Delwin T. / Angela M. Brown, "World Color Survey color naming reveals universal motifs and their within-language diversity," *Psychological and Cognitive Sciences*, PANS, November 24, 2009
https://www.pnas.org/doi/10.1073/pnas.0910981106#con2

Unit 14 Jumping to Conclusions
Shatz, Itamar, "Jumping to Conclusions: When People Decide Based on Insufficient Information," Effectiviology.
https://effectiviology.com/jumping-to-conclusions/

Unit 15 Information Overload
"What is Information Overload?", Interaction Design Foundation.
https://www.interaction-design.org/literature/topics/information-overload
"How to Overcome Information Overload: Complete Guide 101," IvyPanda, Feb 1, 2023.
https://ivypanda.com/blog/information-overload-101/

リーディング・プロスペクト
英文読解(えいぶんどっかい)の総合演習(そうごうえんしゅう)

2024年2月20日　第1版発行

著　者—— 松尾秀樹（まつお　ひでき）
Alexander A. Bodnar（アレクサンダー・A・ボードナー）
Jay C. Stocker（ジェイ・C・ストッカー）
藤本温（ふじもと　つもる）

発行者—— 前田俊秀

発行所—— 株式会社　三修社

〒150-0001
東京都渋谷区神宮前 2-2-22
TEL 03-3405-4511 / FAX 03-3405-4522
振替 00190-9-72758
https://www.sanshusha.co.jp
編集担当　永尾真理

印刷・製本—— 壮光舎印刷株式会社

ISBN978-4-384-33529-3 C1082

DTP —— XYLO
表紙デザイン —— やぶはなあきお